GitLab Quick Start Guide

Migrate to GitLab for all your repository management solutions

Adam O'Grady

BIRMINGHAM - MUMBAI

GitLab Quick Start Guide

Commissioning Editor: Pavan Ramchandani
Acquisition Editor: Aditi Gour
Content Development Editor: Mohammed Yusuf Imaratwale
Technical Editor: Jinesh Topiwala
Copy Editor: Safis Editing
Project Coordinator: Hardik Bhinde
Proofreader: Safis Editing
Indexer: Rekha Nair
Graphics: Jason Monteiro
Production Coordinator: Pratik Shirodkar

First published: November 2018

Production reference: 1291118

Published by Packt Publishing Ltd.
Livery Place
35 Livery Street
Birmingham
B3 2PB, UK.

ISBN 978-1-78953-434-4

www.packtpub.com

To Nikki, Shmouf, and Snowy for their encouragement, support, and snacks.

– Adam O'Grady

`mapt.io`

Mapt is an online digital library that gives you full access to over 5,000 books and videos, as well as industry leading tools to help you plan your personal development and advance your career. For more information, please visit our website.

Why subscribe?

- Spend less time learning and more time coding with practical eBooks and Videos from over 4,000 industry professionals

- Improve your learning with Skill Plans built especially for you

- Get a free eBook or video every month

- Mapt is fully searchable

- Copy and paste, print, and bookmark content

Packt.com

Did you know that Packt offers eBook versions of every book published, with PDF and ePub files available? You can upgrade to the eBook version at `www.packt.com` and as a print book customer, you are entitled to a discount on the eBook copy. Get in touch with us at `customercare@packtpub.com` for more details.

At `www.packt.com`, you can also read a collection of free technical articles, sign up for a range of free newsletters, and receive exclusive discounts and offers on Packt books and eBooks.

Contributors

About the author

Adam O'Grady hails from the remote Perth, Western Australia, and can usually be found on Twitter at @adamjogrady or in meatspace wrangling with code.

His first taste of programming came from building games into graphics calculators at high school, and quickly developed into a passion. A few years later, while doing social media marketing for an ISP, his first big break arrived; building custom applications to monitor and respond to social feeds.

After that, he spent a few years working for the government building systems that used satellite and geographic data to spot and predict bushfires, and now you can find him leading a small team of engineering mavens at a local health start-up.

I couldn't have done this without the love and support of my partner, Nikki. Also deserving of huge shout-outs are Shmouf, my parents, and all my patient and caring friends online and IRL. Props to everyone at iiNet, Landgate, and HealthEngine for giving me chances and helping me succeed.

And especially a massive thanks to Aditi and Mohammed at Packt Publishing for the opportunity to write this and the guidance to finish it.

About the reviewer

Reece Como is an experienced mobile and backend engineer who works in the mobile and growth teams at Australia's largest healthcare platform, HealthEngine. Previously he has worked at The University of Western Australia, assisting with the teaching of networks, security, and cloud computing, under the guidance of Dr. David Glance. Reece, who has a degree in both marketing and computer science, is passionate about finding the real-world applications of technologies, and using them to grow and enrich people's lives.

> *I thank my father and friends for their love and support. Many special thanks to Tara Heath and the team at HealthEngine for the incredible work they put in every day to make healthcare more accessible.*

Packt is searching for authors like you

If you're interested in becoming an author for Packt, please visit `authors.packtpub.com` and apply today. We have worked with thousands of developers and tech professionals, just like you, to help them share their insight with the global tech community. You can make a general application, apply for a specific hot topic that we are recruiting an author for, or submit your own idea.

Table of Contents

Preface

This book explores the GitLab platform, an online system that allows you to host and test code, deploy your application, as well as manage changes, features, bugs, documentation, and much more. We'll explore using the online offering provided by GitLab.com as well as setting up your own GitLab server, creating/importing/editing projects, and testing/deploying your project directly through GitLab.

Who this book is for

This book is geared towards system administrators and developers (and hybrid roles including SREs and DevOps) who are looking to learn more about the GitLab version control/code hosting platform; however, it is usable by anyone who sees a use for version control systems, including authors writing a book or teams looking for a collaborative way to edit large markup files or datasets.

For those just looking to explore GitLab's web user interface, create projects, and edit files online, readers should be comfortable with a web browser and very basic familiarity with the Terminal or command line, including changing directories and listing files in a directory.

Readers who are interested in installing their own GitLab instance must be familiar with using a Unix-based operating system such as Ubuntu or CentOS, including working with the command line and installing software.

People taking advantage of the continuous integration/continuous delivery features of GitLab should be comfortable with their programming language of choice as well as any preferred test suites or linters. The examples in this book use a PHP project, but it is just to demonstrate committing code and setting up tests. It's not a core requirement to know PHP.

What this book covers

Chapter 1, *Introducing GitLab*, is a brief introduction to GitLab and its features. We explore the basic concepts of version control systems and look at Git in particular.

Chapter 2, *Setting Up GitLab*, covers account creation on GitLab and, for those interested in running their own GitLab server, we go into installation and some basic configuration using both the provided Omnibus packages and a manual install.

Chapter 3, *GitLab Flow*, delves further into Git, including how to use it, followed by an older *best practices* workflow for Git projects. This is used to introduce the *GitLab flow*, a method of working with Git and GitLab for increased efficiency and simplicity.

Chapter 4, *Issues to Merge Requests*, gets you acquainted with the GitLab user interface by creating projects, basic project management, and working with merge requests, all demonstrated using an example project.

Chapter 5, *Continuous Integration and Continuous Deployment*, gives you a look at the CI/CD features of GitLab that allow for automated testing and deployment of your applications.

Chapter 6, *Porting from GitHub and Subversion (SVN)*, explains how to migrate from other code hosting platforms and other version control systems.

Chapter 7, *Advanced and Paid Features*, finishes the book by looking at some of the extra parts of GitLab to help you become a power user, while also introducing some of the paid features GitLab provides if you want to consider an enterprise license.

Appendix, *Introduction To Markdown*, we will give you a brief overview on Markdown and how it can be applied at various instances such as Headings, Emphasising content, lists, adding links, images, and creating a block of code.

To get the most out of this book

I recommend having a computer nearby while reading this book so that you can explore the user interface options in GitLab as you go. While knowledge of PHP isn't a prerequisite, it is used in the example project, so passing familiarity is handy. If you've used other object-oriented programming languages before it'll mostly make sense.

Download the example code files

You can download the example code files for this book from your account at
`www.packt.com`. If you purchased this book elsewhere, you can visit
`www.packt.com/support` and register to have the files emailed directly to you.

You can download the code files by following these steps:

1. Log in or register at `www.packt.com`.
2. Select the **SUPPORT** tab.
3. Click on **Code Downloads & Errata**.
4. Enter the name of the book in the **Search** box and follow the onscreen
   instructions.

Once the file is downloaded, please make sure that you unzip or extract the folder using the
latest version of:

- WinRAR/7-Zip for Windows
- Zipeg/iZip/UnRarX for Mac
- 7-Zip/PeaZip for Linux

The code bundle for the book is also hosted on GitHub at `https://github.com/
PacktPublishing/GitLab-Quick-Start-Guide`. In case there's an update to the code, it will
be updated on the existing GitHub repository.

We also have other code bundles from our rich catalog of books and videos available
at `https://github.com/PacktPublishing/`. Check them out!

Download the color images

We also provide a PDF file that has color images of the screenshots/diagrams used in this
book. You can download it
here: `https://www.packtpub.com/sites/default/files/downloads/9781789534344_Color
Images.pdf`.

Conventions used

There are a number of text conventions used throughout this book.

`CodeInText`: Indicates code words in text, database table names, folder names, filenames, file extensions, pathnames, dummy URLs, user input, and Twitter handles. Here is an example: "Firstly we need to update the `external_url` value in our `/etc/gitlab /gitlab.rb` file to reference HTTPS."

A block of code is set as follows:

```php
<?php
namespace Judges119\Monolog\Formatter;
use Monolog\Formatter\FormatterInterface;
class ROT13Formatter implements FormatterInterface
{
public function format(array $record)
{
return str_rot13($record['message']);
}
public function formatBatch(array $records)
{
foreach ($records as $key => $record) {
$records[$key] = $this->format($record);
}
return $records;
}
}
```

Any command-line input or output is written as follows:

```
sudo apt-get update
sudo apt-get install -y curl openssh-server ca-certificates
```

Bold: Indicates a new term, an important word, or words that you see onscreen. For example, words in menus or dialog boxes appear in the text like this. Here is an example: "The last section of interest to us is **Environments**.
By clicking on **Operations** | **Environments** through the menu on the left "

Warnings or important notes appear like this.

Tips and tricks appear like this.

Get in touch

Feedback from our readers is always welcome.

General feedback: If you have questions about any aspect of this book, mention the book title in the subject of your message and email us at customercare@packtpub.com.

Errata: Although we have taken every care to ensure the accuracy of our content, mistakes do happen. If you have found a mistake in this book, we would be grateful if you would report this to us. Please visit www.packt.com/submit-errata, selecting your book, clicking on the Errata Submission Form link, and entering the details.

Piracy: If you come across any illegal copies of our works in any form on the Internet, we would be grateful if you would provide us with the location address or website name. Please contact us at copyright@packt.com with a link to the material.

If you are interested in becoming an author: If there is a topic that you have expertise in and you are interested in either writing or contributing to a book, please visit authors.packtpub.com.

Reviews

Please leave a review. Once you have read and used this book, why not leave a review on the site that you purchased it from? Potential readers can then see and use your unbiased opinion to make purchase decisions, we at Packt can understand what you think about our products, and our authors can see your feedback on their book. Thank you!

For more information about Packt, please visit packt.com.

Introducing GitLab

1

GitLab is a code hosting and issue tracking web platform based around the Git version control system. First released in 2011, it has continued to grow and evolve over the years, adding new features and capabilities, and has turned into a one-stop tool for an agile workforce. While it is owned and managed by GitLab Inc., who steer the direction of the project, the core of GitLab is open source software with over 2,000 separate contributors to date.

In this chapter, we'll explore the following topics:

- An overview of version control
- The main features of GitLab
- Self-managed versus SaaS
- Free versus paid
- A brief history of GitLab

Version control systems and Git

Let's say you write code, or work on a book, or even just want to collect and update a set of text-based documents. You need some method of keeping track of changes, of being able to revert mistakes in the work, or branch in new directions; and you'll probably want some way of remotely backing up your work in case of fire, theft, or acts of a misbehaving computer. This is where version control systems (also known as VCS) come in handy. They save your work at certain points (**commits**) and can be reverted to earlier states; many VCS offer methods of **branching** so that you can – for example – work on a specific feature without interrupting someone else's work on another component. There are many version control systems on the market, but the most prominent in the public eye would be Git. Git is a distributed version control system, which means that it has a full copy of all of the code that exists on each user's computer, and users can pass patches and changes directly between each other rather than entirely relying on a centralized server.

Behind the scenes, git is an advanced program that is lightning fast when it comes to performing operations like staging work, committing changes, or swapping between branches. It's efficient at fetching information from remote repositories to help speed up a user's workflow. Unlike most VCS, git doesn't work by storing the changes that happen to each file. Instead, on every commit, git stores a snapshot of the current state of all files. If a file hasn't changed, rather than storing it again, it simply stores a reference to the last saved version of the file.

When you make a commit, git captures the snapshot and also takes a **cryptographic hash** – a series of complex mathematical operations on the data that produces a unique value – and uses the output of that as a reference to the commit, along with some metadata, such as the author. This snapshot sits on top of the rest of the snapshots/commits that you've taken, and in this way you can think of git snapshots as a series of changesets – operations that add or remove lines – that can be performed on your files to get them to an older or newer state.

We'll cover more on the higher-level use and commands of Git in `Chapter 3`, *GitLab Flow*, when we explore the GitLab flow for branching and merging.

GitLab and Git

GitLab is built on top of git so that users who are contributing work (editing code, writing chapters, and so on) to a project will have a copy of the project downloaded/checked out/cloned on their local computer. It provides a web interface for handling many of git's more advanced workflows, and recommends a workflow for interacting with git for the best in productivity, efficiency, and ease of use. We'll cover this workflow in a lot more detail in `Chapter 3`, *GitLab Flow*, and in `Chapter 4`, *Issues to Merge Requests*, where we'll explore the merging of branches in the GitLab user interface.

By acting as a single source of truth for your developers, GitLab can help you avoid conflicts and the double handling of work while maintaining uptime by relying on the battle-tested `GitLab.com` platform or your own installation of it, working with tools including geographic replication, disaster recovery, and automated failover.

Features

GitLab provides a number of ways to view and interact with a git repository. There is the classic file browser that lets you explore the files in your repository:

📁 shared	Add GitLab Pages	1 year ago
📁 spec	Merge remote-tracking branch 'dev/master'	10 hours ago
📁 symbol	Resolve "Better SVG Usage in the Frontend"	10 months ago
📁 tmp	Move Prometheus presentation logic to Prometh...	1 year ago
📁 vendor	Specify Jupyter Image to use with JupyterHub In...	6 days ago
📄 .babelrc	only apply rewire plugin when running karma tests	3 months ago
📄 .codeclimate.yml	Removed API endpoint and specs	1 month ago
📄 .csscomb.json	Remove SCSS rules for short hex chars.	1 year ago
📄 .eslintignore	update eslintignore for node scripts	4 months ago
📄 .eslintrc.yml	Enable "prefer-destructuring" in JS files	1 month ago
📄 .flayignore	Backport from EE !5954	3 weeks ago
📄 .foreman	complete hooks for post receive	6 years ago
📄 .gitattributes	Start to use Danger for automating MR reviews	2 weeks ago
📄 .gitignore	Exclude Geo DB Yaml on CE too	1 month ago

There's also a branch viewer, which lets you see variations of your work under active development, as well as branches that are considered stale and no longer developed:

Alongside this is a tag viewer that lets you explore specific releases of your work:

There are tools that can be used to analyze and view the commit graph:

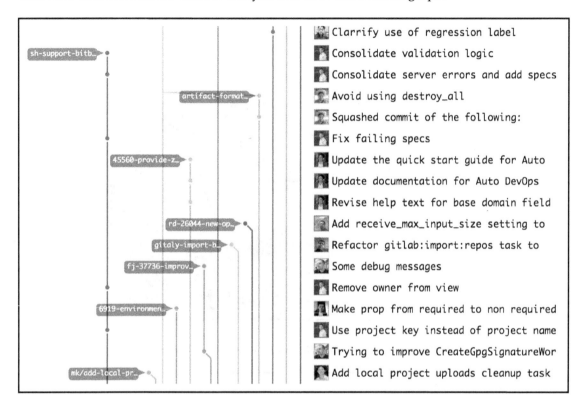

Among these tools are charting tools, which are used to get a better understanding of the composition of the repository:

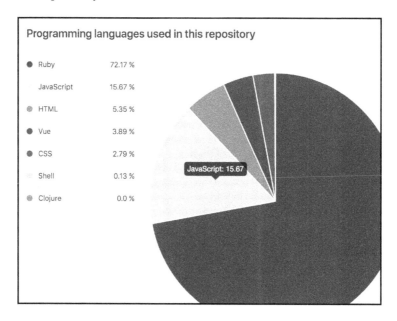

Alongside this is a breakdown of the frequencies of commits and activity:

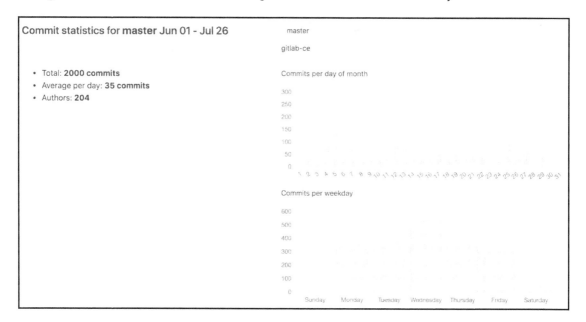

For users who are not familiar with git commands or those away from their work computer, GitLab also provides a web interface where you can make changes to code and commit it straight from the browser:

Aside from being a web interface for git, GitLab also provides tools for a variety of purposes, including powerful feature planning and issue management tools:

These tools help keep everyone in sync, allowing them to understand the current workload and roadmap and making sure that work isn't double-handled and is correctly prioritized. With things like epics, milestones, and cycle analytics, GitLab can help measure the effectiveness of your development process.

It also includes the necessary tools for code review prior to merging branches to ensure that all work is up to scratch:

Automated testing tools and pipelines are also included to help make sure that code is working perfectly before it's merged back in or released:

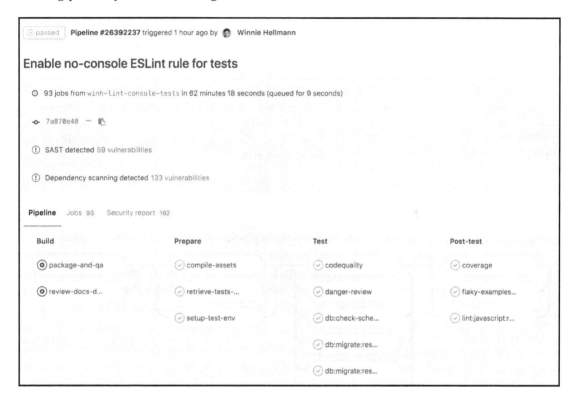

Thanks to the powerful, built-in, continuous integration/continuous deployment (CI/CD) platform (explored further in `Chapter 5`, *Continuous Integration And Continuous Deployment*), GitLab can not only test your code, but also build and deploy/release it under circumstances that you control.

Self-managed versus Software as a Service (SaaS)

GitLab can be used in one of two ways: either self-managed, where you host your own instance of GitLab Community Edition/Enterprise Edition, or using the online platform `GitLab.com`, which comes as a paid or free **Software as a Service (SaaS)** model.

Using `GitLab.com` comes with the benefits of no maintenance or infrastructure costs and regular automatic updates without any manual labour. They have an amazing setup with multiple backup strategies, redundancies, and failovers to ensure high uptime and no loss of data in the event of a major incident.

On the other hand, you might not feel comfortable putting all of your work on someone else's infrastructure, which is why GitLab provides an easy-to-install omnibus package that can be installed on your own computer or a server that you host. This can also be handy if you have strict security and firewall requirements that don't allow for externally hosted code. There's also the benefit of easy integration with your own LDAP or Active Directory services for user management, and potential performance gains in larger repositories from not having to shift large amounts of data over external network links.

Free versus paid

Lastly, there are multiple tiers of GitLab for both the self-managed and SaaS versions. Please note that both versions can be used for free and provide all of the main features that you'd expect (git hosting, code review, issue management, testing, and deployment). The added tiers provide extra features that are available at different levels of pricing on a per-user, per-month basis. For example, at the lowest paid tier, you get priority and next-business-day support, and with the SaaS version, you also get burndown charts, multiple approval requirements on merge requests, and issue weighting. At the higher levels, more features get added, including the following:

- Service desk mode
- Canary deployments
- Support for multiple Kubernetes clusters
- CI/CD for external repositories
- Disaster recovery
- Epics
- Roadmaps, and much more

We'll cover more of these paid features in `Chapter 7`, *Advanced and Paid Features*.

Summary

So far, we've discovered what version control is: a method of tracking revisions of work, of creating alternate test branches, and working collaboratively. We know that git is a form of version control system that specializes in working in a distributed network and that GitLab is a platform that is based on git but with a lot of powerful features.

We discussed the features of GitLab, including issue and project management, continuous integration and continuous deployment, code review, and even online code editing. We also looked at self-managed GitLab versus using the online `GitLab.com` platform. You should also have an idea of the benefits of moving to a paid GitLab subscription.

In the next chapter, we'll discuss setting up GitLab for self-managed users, and go over both the quick omnibus installation and the manual installation method. We'll also look into how to create an account on a GitLab instance, whether a self-managed one or on `GitLab.com`.

2
Setting Up GitLab

As discussed in the previous chapter, GitLab can be used both as a self-managed or as a SaaS offering through GitLab.com. We also discussed the reasons for and against both methods regarding getting started with GitLab. We'll start this chapter by running through the requirements of GitLab, and in particular what you need in terms of hardware and software to run your own installation. The onnibus package and its installation on Ubuntu and CentOS will be investigated, as well as manual installations for people who can't install the omnibus package. We'll also look at a few ways of setting up an installation, as well as how to set up an account on your new installation or on GitLab.com. In particular, we'll cover the following topics:

- Requirements
- Omnibus installation on Ubuntu
- Omnibus installation on CentOS
- Manual installation on Ubuntu
- Setting up HTTPS
- Creating an account on GitLab.com

Requirements

Let's take a quick look at what operating system and hardware you will need to get GitLab up and running.

Hardware

In general, you'll want a minimum of two physical CPU cores to handle about 500 total users. This is feasible with one core, but you'll have the workers and background jobs running on the same core, which might slow things down. Above that, four cores will support about 2,000 users, and if you need any more than 40,000 users (which will run fine on 64 cores), you should probably look at running multiple application servers at once.

For memory, the recommendation is 2 GB of RAM, which will easily support 100 users with no issue. 1 GB of physical memory with 1 GB of swap space is probably the bare minimum you can get away with; it'll work okay with a small number of users, but can get quite slow. This would be appropriate for a tiny private instance for you and some friends or a fledgling start up. Any less RAM and you'll start getting some strange 5 xx errors being thrown during use and other errors if you try and reconfigure. You can also scale up to 2,000 users with 16 GB of RAM and upwards to 32,000 users on a beastly 256 GB server. Again, any more users required than that and you should probably be running multiple application servers.

Storage-wise, you'll definitely need enough space to handle all of your repositories combined (about 10-100 MB for many projects). On top of that, you'll have your database, which needs about 1 MB of space per user and will grow with time and more project involvement. Mostly, though, you'll need space for your operating system and all of the applications required by GitLab, so having at least 5-10 GB free is a good starting point.

Operating system

GitLab provides an **omnibus** package for installation on a number of platforms. This package has everything required to run a full-fledged GitLab instance, including the database (PostgreSQL), in-memory caching platform (Redis), background task queue (Sidekiq), and monitoring platform (Prometheus). This is the recommended way of installing GitLab for most circumstances, unless you are setting up for a massive instance, want more fine-grained control over the components, are looking to run your own public code hosting platform, use an unsupported Unix-based OS, or are reusing other equipment and servers. The omnibus package is currently available for the following operating systems:

- Ubuntu
- Debian
- CentOS
- OpenSUSE

- Red Hat Enterprise Linux (RHEL)
- Scientific Linux
- Oracle Linux

If your operating system flavor of choice hasn't been mentioned, there is still the option of a manual installation, which has been tested on distributions including the following:

- Arch Linux
- Fedora
- FreeBSD
- Gentoo
- mac OS

Please note that GitLab is not supported on non-Unix operating systems such as Windows, OS/2 Warp, or Plan Nine.

Languages and applications

The core application of GitLab is based on Ruby and requires at least Ruby 2.3. Unfortunately, for fans of Ruby variants such as JRuby or Rubinius, GitLab relies on several gems (additional libraries) that have native extensions and thus relies on Ruby MRI (Matz's Ruby Interpreter).

This is the only extra requirement if you plan on using the omnibus installation package. However, if you're looking to install manually, there are a few other requirements to get your head around.

First, you'll need a relational database; GitLab very highly recommends and is designed around PostgreSQL. However, in a bind, MySQL can be supported but with a few less features and a reduced experience (no geo replication or load balancing, no zero downtime migrations, and unoptimized dashboard loading). For PostgreSQL users, you should be on at least version 9.6 as this is what they use for development and testing; they can't guarantee compatibility with older versions.

The GitLab team only supports the last three releases of major browsers, and includes the following:

- Google Chrome
- Mozilla Firefox
- macOS Safari
- Microsoft Edge
- Microsoft Internet Explorer 11

It's also important to be wary of the fact that GitLab must have JavaScript enabled in order to work in the web browser. Disabling it cannot guarantee that any part of the site will work since support for JS is baked into the core of the platform.

Omnibus on Ubuntu/Debian

To install GitLab using the omnibus package on an Ubuntu or Debian system, make sure that you have a server with one of the following versions installed on it:

- Ubuntu 14.04 LTS
- Ubuntu 16.04 LTS
- Ubuntu 18.04 LTS
- Debian 7
- Debian 8
- Debian 9

While the installation may work on other systems, it isn't guaranteed.

First, you'll need to connect to a Terminal session, update your package lists, and make sure that a few key packages are installed by running the following commands:

```
sudo apt-get update
sudo apt-get install -y curl openssh-server ca-certificates
```

Next, you'll need to decide whether you want to use Postfix to send notification emails or an external SMTP provider. While the latter is recommended, if you do plan to use Postfix, you'll need to install it like so:

```
sudo apt-get install -y postfix
```

During the installation of Postfix, a configuration screen will appear. Make sure that you select **Internet Site** and set an appropriate mail name (preferably the server's external DNS name). For any other requests, you can accept the defaults.

Next, you'll need to add the GitLab package repository. There's a simple way to do this that's been provided by GitLab, and that's by running the following command:

```
curl
https://packages.gitlab.com/install/repositories/gitlab/gitlab-ee/script.de
b.sh | sudo bash
```

If you feel uncomfortable cURLing directly from the internet into a shell, you can download the shell script, inspect it, and run it, or browse to it and then run the commands individually.

> While it is innocuous in this case, it's a good security practice to be wary about running shell scripts straight form the internet, especially to an elevated/administrator command prompt. They could contain anything, including malicious commands.

Now, you'll want to install the GitLab package. To do to this, you should run the following command, supplementing `http://example.com` with the URL or IP you plan to use for this installation. This command will configure and start the GitLab instance for you automatically:

```
sudo EXTERNAL_URL="http://example.com" apt-get install gitlab-ee
```

Once the installation has completed, you should be faced with the following Terminal output:

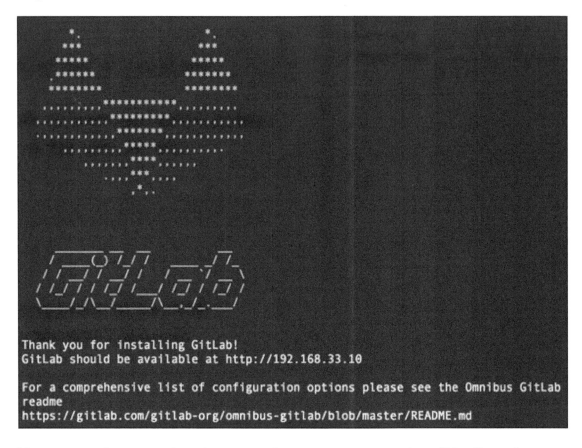

Now, you can browse to the value you set for EXTERNAL_URL and you'll be directed to a password setup screen:

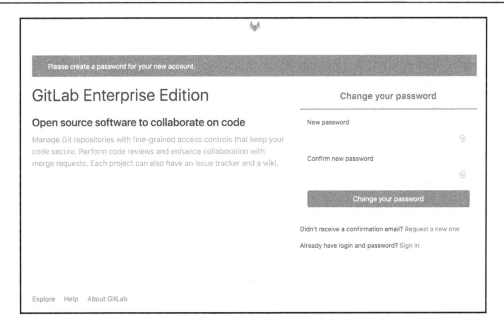

Provide a password and you'll be directed to log in. Use the account name `root` and the password you just set and you'll be all set up:

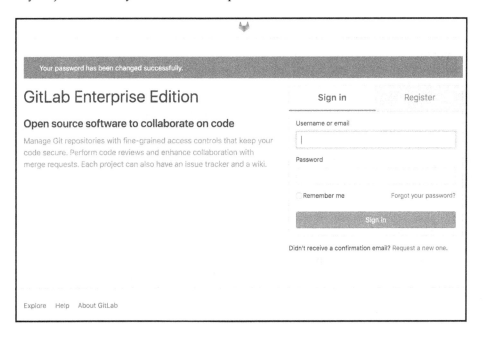

Omnibus on CentOS/RHEL/Scientific Linux/Oracle Linux

To install GitLab using the omnibus package on a CentOS, Red Hat Enterprise Linux (RHEL), Scientific Linux, or Oracle Linux system, make sure that you have a server with a base that's compatible with CentOS 7.

First, you'll need to connect to a Terminal session and make sure that a few key packages are installed by running the following commands:

```
sudo yum install -y curl policycoreutils-python openssh-server
```

Now, you'll need to allow HTTP and SSH traffic through the local device firewall. This can be done by running the following code lines:

```
sudo systemctl enable sshd
sudo systemctl start sshd
sudo firewall-cmd --permanent --add-service=http
sudo systemctl reload firewalld
```

Next, you'll need to decide on whether you want to use Postfix to send notification emails or external SMTP provider. While the latter is recommended, if you do plan to use Postfix, you'll need to install it like so:

```
sudo yum install postfix
sudo systemctl enable postfix
sudo systemctl start postfix
```

During the installation of Postfix, a configuration screen will appear. Make sure that you select **Internet Site** and set an appropriate mail name (preferably the server's external DNS name). For any other requests, you can accept the defaults.

Next, you'll need to add the GitLab package repository. There's a simple way to do this, and that's by running the following command:

```
curl
https://packages.gitlab.com/install/repositories/gitlab/gitlab-ee/script.rp
m.sh | sudo bash
```

If you feel uncomfortable cURLing directly from the internet into a shell, you can download the shell script, inspect it, and run it, or browse to it and then run the commands individually.

While it is innocuous in this case, it's a good security practice to be wary about running shell scripts straight form the internet, especially to an elevated/administrator command prompt. They could contain anything, including malicious commands.

Now, you'll want to install the GitLab package. To do to this, you should run the following command, supplementing `http://example.com` with the URL or IP you plan to use for this installation. This command will configure and start the GitLab instance for you automatically:

```
sudo EXTERNAL_URL="http://example.com" yum install -y gitlab-ee
```

Once the installation has completed, you should be faced with the following terminal output:

Now, you can browse to the value you set for EXTERNAL_URL and you'll be directed to a password setup screen:

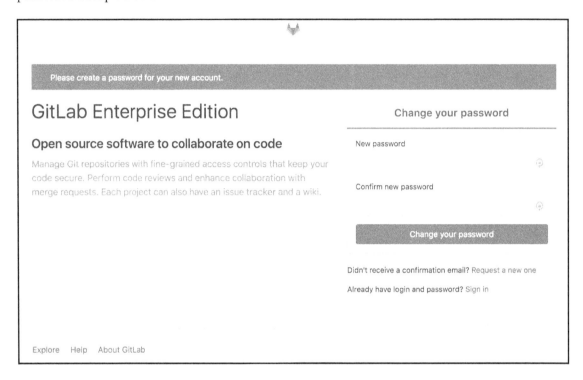

Provide a password and you'll be directed to log in. Use the account name root and the password you just set and you'll be all set up:

Manual installation

There are some situations where you won't be able to use an omnibus package to install GitLab, potentially if you want to use your own existing hardware, existing server software, or your own database. In these cases, you can do a manual installation of GitLab, which we will run through in this section. Please be aware that it is a more complicated process, and using the omnibus installation package is recommended if possible.

Initial packages

There are some initial packages you'll need to install before you even think about language runtimes. Many might be available through your chosen operating system's package manager, otherwise you might need to source them from the net. The current list is as follows:

- gcc
- g++
- libc
- make
- curl
- openssh-server
- logrotate
- rsync
- cmake
- zlib development library
- yaml development library
- ssl development library
- GDBM development library
- GNU readline development library
- ncurses 5 development library
- libffi development library
- XML development library
- XSLT development library
- curl SSL development library
- ICU development library
- RE2 development library

If you're on a system with the apt package manager, such as Ubuntu or Debian, all of these packages can be installed by using the following code:

```
sudo apt-get install -y build-essential zlib1g-dev libyaml-dev libssl-dev
libgdbm-dev libreadline-dev libncurses5-dev libffi-dev curl openssh-server
libxml2-dev libxslt-dev libcurl4-openssl-dev libicu-dev logrotate rsync
python-docutils pkg-config cmake libre2-dev
```

Languages, frameworks, and Git

First, you'll need to install Ruby 2.3.x. You can use a packaged version if your OS has one or you may have to compile it from the source (available at https://www.ruby-lang.org/en/). GitLab advises against using a version manager such as RVM, rbenv, and chruby as they can have problems interacting with the GitLab shell once it's been called from OpenSSH. After Ruby has been installed, install the Bundler gem with the following command:

```
sudo gem install bundler
```

Next up, there's Go. Used for several daemons and services, you can download this directly from the Go home page (https://golang.org/dl/) and follow their guides to getting started.

Node.js is used for compiling assets used by GitLab, and Yarn is used for managing JavaScript dependencies. You need at least version 6.0.0 of Node (https://nodejs.org/en/download/package-manager/) and 12.0.0 of Yarn (https://yarnpkg.com/en/docs/install/#mac-stable) to get this all working.

Now, you'll need to create a Git user for GitLab with the following command; remember the password you choose:

```
sudo adduser --gecos 'GitLab' git
```

Databases

As discussed in the *Requirements* section, PostgreSQL is the database that's recommended by GitLab for running with full feature availability. You can find out how to download it from the PostgreSQL website at https://www.postgresql.org/download/.

Once installed, connect to the database via a psql session with an admin user and run the following commands:

```
CREATE USER git CREATEDB;
CREATE EXTENSION IF NOT EXISTS pg_trgm; -- Enables an extension required by
GitLab
CREATE DATABASE gitlabhq_production OWNER git;
```

Now, you should have your database set up. First, we'll need to log in and set a password for this user:

```
sudo -u git -H psql gitlabhq_production
\password
```

Exit the database connection with \q and move on to the other main datastore, Redis. It may be available in your OS package manager (assuming that one is available), otherwise you can find installation instructions on the Redis website at https://redis.io/download:

```
sed 's/^port .*/port 0/' /etc/redis/redis.conf.orig | sudo tee
/etc/redis/redis.conf

# Enable Redis socket
echo 'unixsocket /var/run/redis/redis.sock' | sudo tee -a
/etc/redis/redis.conf

# Grant permission to the socket to all members of the group
echo 'unixsocketperm 770' | sudo tee -a /etc/redis/redis.conf

# Create the directory which contains the socket
mkdir /var/run/redis
sudo chown redis:redis /var/run/redis
sudo chmod 755 /var/run/redis

# Persist the directory which contains the socket, if applicable
if [ -d /etc/tmpfiles.d ]; then
 echo 'd /var/run/redis 0755 redis redis 10d -' | sudo tee -a
/etc/tmpfiles.d/redis.conf
fi

# Add git to the redis group
sudo usermod -aG redis git
```

You'll need to restart the Redis server and it should be good to go.

GitLab

Now, we're finally ready to install GitLab itself! Log in (or use su) as the git user and check out the GitLab Community Edition repository:

1. Make sure that you go to the GitLab website first and pick a branch that's new and stable, like I have in the following code:

```
git clone https://gitlab.com/gitlab-org/gitlab-ce.git -b 11-1-stable
gitlab
```

2. Next up, change into the directory that you just checked GitLab into:

```
cd gitlab
```

3. Copy the example `config` and edit the file with your preferred text editor, according to the directions at the top of the file:

```
cp config/gitlab.yml.example config/gitlab.yml
```

4. Make the uploads directory:

```
mkdir public/uploads/
```

5. Copy the default config files:

```
cp config/secrets.yml.example config/secrets.yml
cp config/unicorn.rb.example config/unicorn.rb
cp config/initializers/rack_attack.rb.example config/initializers
/rack_attack.rb
cp config/resque.yml.example config/resque.yml
cp config/database.yml.postgresql config/database.yml
```

6. Edit `config/database.yml` with your preferred text editor and update the production | password value with your git user password.

7. Configure the global `git` settings:

```
git config --global core.autocrlf input
git config --global gc.auto 0
git config --global repack.writeBitmaps true
git config --global receive.advertisePushOptions true
```

8. Install gems:

```
bundle install —deployment
```

9. Install GitLab Shell:

```
bundle exec rake gitlab:shell:install
REDIS_URL=unix:/var/run/redis/redis.sock RAILS_ENV=production
SKIP_STORAGE_VALIDATION=true
```

10. Install GitLab Workhorse:

```
bundle exec rake "gitlab:workhorse:install[/home/git/gitlab-
workhorse]" RAILS_ENV=production
```

11. Install Gitaly:

```
bundle exec rake "gitlab:gitaly:install[/home/git/gitaly]"
RAILS_ENV=production
```

12. Install GitLab (answer `yes` to any questions):

    ```
    bundle exec rake gitlab:setup RAILS_ENV=production
    ```

13. Check the status of GitLab:

    ```
    bundle exec rake gitlab:env:info RAILS_ENV=production
    ```

14. Prepare and compile the assets:

    ```
    bundle exec rake gettext:compile RAILS_ENV=production
    yarn install --production --pure-lockfile
    bundle exec rake gitlab:assets:compile RAILS_ENV=production
    NODE_ENV=production
    ```

15. Start GitLab:

    ```
    lib/support/init.d/gitlab start
    ```

Installing nginx

The last thing we have to do is set up a web server. The server that's recommended by GitLab is nginx, at least version 1.12.1. Once you have it installed, set up the config:

```
sudo cp /home/git/gitlab/lib/support/nginx/gitlab /etc/nginx/sites-available/gitlab
sudo ln -s /etc/nginx/sites-available/gitlab /etc/nginx/sites-enabled/gitlab
```

Now, you'll need to edit that config in your preferred text editor to update the YOUR_SERVER_FQDN value to match the hostname you'll be using for GitLab.

Finally, you should be all done and able to browse to the URL for GitLab that you set, and create a password to log in.

Setting up HTTPS

Security-conscious readers may have picked up that we're only using insecure HTTP, which might be fine for local installs or air-gapped networks, but if you're running on a cloud server, want to protect your server from man-in-the-middle attacks, or just want to follow best practices, I've outlined two ways that you can implement HTTPS. The first involves the free Let's Encrypt SSL provider and the second one is an option if you have your own certificates ready to go.

Let's Encrypt

GitLab comes with the ability to automatically fetch and renew certificates from Let's Encrypt for the primary domain and the container registry for you. To get this running, you just need to specify `https://` for your external URL while setting up GitLab. Make sure that you don't have any custom SSL certificates loaded (this is discussed in the next section).

 Let's Encrypt is a free, automated, and open Certificate Authority.

If you want to receive notification emails about the certificate expiring soon, you can also add the following line to your `/etc/gitlab/gitlab.rb` file:

```
letsencrypt['contact_emails'] = ['foo@example.com']
```

Make sure to replace `foo@example.com` with your actual email address and then run the following command to reconfigure GitLab with the updated information:

```
sudo gitlab-ctl reconfigure
```

If you want to automatically redirect any HTTP traffic to HTTPS, you can add the following line to your GitLab config file (`/etc/gitlab/gitlab.rb`) and then run `sudo gitlab-ctl reconfigure`:

```
nginx['redirect_http_to_https'] = true
```

HTTPS certificates

So far, we've discussed using HTTP with a new GitLab installation and automatically configuring GitLab with HTTPS using Let's Encrypt, but if you have manual certificates you want to use – potentially if your installation won't support Let's Encrypt, is behind a firewall, or on a private network – you can still configure GitLab to use SSL/TLS security to secure HTTP browsing.

First, we need to update the `external_url` value in our `/etc/gitlab/gitlab.rb` file to reference HTTPS:

```
external_url "https://example.com"
```

This lets GitLab know how to use key and certificate files. First, it tries to look for them in `/etc/gitlab/ssl/`. Then, it tries to look for `.key` and `.crt` files that match the `external_url` value; in our case, we should call our files `example.com.key` and `example.com.crt` and put them in the aforementioned directory. You may need to create the directory if it doesn't already exist. Now, run the following command to reconfigure your GitLab installation so that you can use HTTPS with your provided certificate:

```
sudo gitlab-ctl reconfigure
```

If you ever replace the certificates without changing the GitLab configuration, you'll need to run the following command to force a reload of nginx so that it picks up the new certificate and key. You can do this like so:

```
sudo gitlab-ctl hup nginx
```

If you want to automatically redirect any HTTP traffic to HTTPS, you can add the following line to your GitLab config file (`/etc/gitlab/gitlab.rb`) and then run `sudo gitlab-ctl reconfigure`:

```
nginx['redirect_http_to_https'] = true
```

Creating accounts on GitLab

Whether you've decided to create your own instance of GitLab or sign up via `GitLab.com`, you'll need to create a personal account. This is super simple to do: you just need to browse to `https://gitlab.com/users/sign_in` (replacing `gitlab.com` with your own instance hostname) and select `Register`.

From here, you need to supply a name, username, email, and password, accept the terms and conditions, and then register. You'll be sent an email with a confirmation link that you can click on to finish activating your account.

Now, you should be ready to move on to the next chapter and explore the GitLab workflow.

Summary

In this chapter, we explored the requirements of GitLab and discovered what systems it can run on. We noted down the required RAM, CPU, storage space, operating system, and software components/frameworks.

We ran through installing and configuring GitLab. We looked at setting up the omnibus package, which is an all-in-one option for getting up and running with GitLab on Ubuntu, CentOS, and their related operating systems.

For people who aren't able to run the Omnibus package, we also ran through a manual installation.

Lastly, we explored creating an account on GitLab.com or a self-managed GitLab instance.

In the next chapter, we'll discover more about git and the workflow that's recommended for projects that are using it. We'll also go through the GitLab workflow, an alternative that was presented by GitLab as the preferred way to work with git projects.

3
GitLab Flow

It's one thing to have platforms and tools like GitLab at your fingertips and another to be able to use them effectively and efficiently to improve your work.

In this chapter, we'll explore the following topics:

- How to use Git
- The GitFlow for branching and merging
- The GitLab flow (recommended by GitLab)
- The GitLab flow in comparison to the GitHub flow

Using Git

In the first chapter, we explored the concept of version control systems and introduced Git as a tool for distributed version control. We also looked briefly at how Gitworks under the hood. However, so far, we haven't explored how to use git, which is a major prerequisite for most users who'll be working with GitLab.

One thing to recognize is the life cycle of Git work and the stages it can go through. There are four separate parts: your working directory, the index or staging area, committing to the local repository, and pushing to remote repositories:

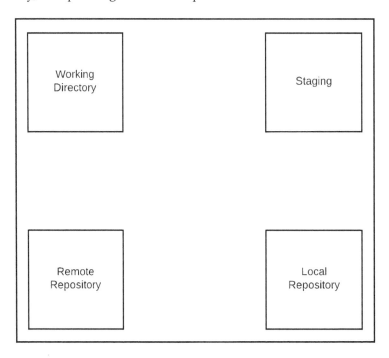

The working directory or working copy consists of your local files and any changes you've made to them. The working directory is created from your commit history by git, which reconstructs it from its storage of blobs (binary large objects). When you change branches, Git looks in its database for the reference to that branch, finds all of the related objects, and turns them back into files for you to view and edit.

Next up are the index or staged files. These get added to when you run `git add` and can be thought of as a preview of your next commit. What happens behind the scenes is this: Githas a file called the index, which can be visualized as a list of all the available files in the working copy, their modification times, and three sets of references. When you run `git add`, it creates blob objects representing the changes and stores them, keeping a reference to the blobs representing the changes made. This way, you can continue editing a file, but when you commit, only the changes up to when you ran `git add` will be kept. The reference is known as the index reference, but the index files also keep a reference to the local copy version and the working copy version so that when it does a checksum over a file, it can tell if it's changed from the index version of the local copy version.

The local repository or local copy version of your Gitrepository represents the committed code. This is a database of all the commits, branches, references, and so on, and a library of all the blobs representing changes and files. When you run `git commit`, all of the changes from the working copy are stored as a reference in this database, and you can start working on new changes again.

Lastly, we have the remote repository. This is a copy of the repository that is held by someone else, whether on a coworker's computer or a code hosting platform such as GitLab. When you run a `git push` command, your changes are packaged and sent over the wire or air to the other repository, where they are integrated. You can also run a `git pull` command, which reaches out to a local repository and grabs any changes that have been made in those repositories that are not yet mirrored in your local copy.

Overall, it seems like a pretty complicated workflow, which is why I've created this handy graph to illustrate the basic operations that you can perform and how they relate to these stages:

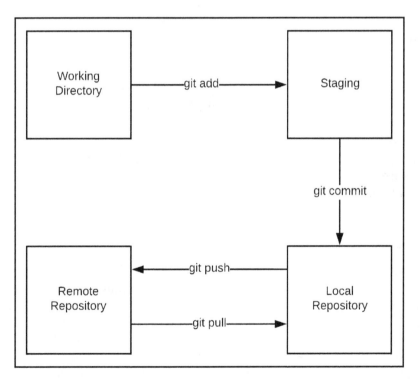

Git commands

I've introduced a few Git commands while discussing how Gitworks, but haven't actually explained properly how to use them, so let's do a very brief introduction to the basic usage of Git.

The first command you'll need when starting a new project is `git init`. This initializes a new Gitrepository, and you'll notice that it creates a `.git` folder so that you can start your project (this is hidden by default on Unix-based and Windows operating systems).

The other situation you might find yourself in is working on an existing project and needing to create a local repository. This can be done with the `git clone` command. You specify a URL with a protocol (such as `https://` or `git://`) and Gitfetches all of the information for that repository before putting it in a folder for that project. It also constructs a working copy from the latest commit on master so that you can begin working on the files immediately.

`git add` is logically the next command you might need when you've changed some files or added a new file to the project. As discussed previously, this adds it to the staging area/index, but there's some neat ways you can go about this. By itself, it returns a snarky message saying **Nothing specified, nothing added.**, but you can supply a file path after that to add a particular file to the index. You can also supply a period (`git add .`) and it'll add all of the files in the current directory to the index. You can also use the asterisk character as a wildcard, for example, `git add meerkats/*`, which adds all of the files in the `meerkats` directory to the staging area, but nothing else. You can also specify a number of file paths, separating them with spaces. If you need to add a file path that contains a space, make sure that you surround it in quotation marks so as not to confuse the poor program. Lastly, you can also run `git add -i` to run an interactive prompt, which shows you the status of the working copy and index and lets you choose files to stage or unstage. It even lets you patch files, selectively staging only parts of the changes you've made rather than the entire file.

Why would we need all of these different ways of adding filautomatically merge your changes with the remote repository es to staging? One common reason is to separate the work that's been done into separate commits with identifying comments/messages so that people looking over the history of the repository have a better understanding of what each chunk of changes meant without having to view the changelogs individually. Another common reason is just to break up a really large change into multiple bite-sized chunks for easy reviewing. You may also have important secrets, configuration files, compiled work, or vendor libraries that you don't want to commit with your code and so you can avoid adding those files into your staging area or local repository.

`git commit` will allow you to commit all of the files you put into staging to the local repository. Since staging has already created the blobs representing the content of your files, all it needs to do is save the index state into the Gitdatabase and then you're ready to go again. It's recommended that you run this command as `git commit -m "MESSAGE"`, replacing the content in the quotation marks with a relevant message to help future collaborators (and future you) understand your thought process behind the commit.

As mentioned previously, `git push` will take your local content and *push* it to a remote repository, whether that's another colleague's computer or a code hosting platform like GitLab. You can do this by specifying `git push <remote> <branch>`. You have to configure a remote repository first, which you can do with `git remote add origin <url>`. Make sure that the URL has the protocol as well (`git://`, `https://`, and so on). You can also change out `origin` for another name if you want to have multiple remote repositories. We'll look at branching or branch commands shortly, but until then you can use `git push origin master` to push the main stream of work to your main configured remote repository. You can also run `git push origin --all` to push all of your local changes on different branches to the remote repositories. One thing to keep in mind is that Gitwill automatically merge your changes with the remote repository as long as your local copy is ahead of the remote repository. If there are later commits on the remote repository than your local copy, the merge will fail because, by default, Gitwon't let you rewrite the history of a repository, only append new data to it.

You can use `git pull` to fetch any remote changes and automatically integrate them into the current repository. Be warned: if there are any conflicts with content coming from the remote repository, you'll need to resolve them before continuing.

If we have multiple people working on the same project and committing/sharing code, how can we prevent them from getting out of sync with each other's copies and then being unable to merge remote changes? This is where branching comes in handy. The git branch command can be specified with a branch name such as git branch 53-changing-font-colour. This will create a new branch called **53-changing-font-colour** that you can then swap to and work on separately from the main code. Once you're done, you could merge this code back into the master branch. Git relies heavily on its lightweight branching model to prevent conflicts and allow for better collaboration. Behind the scenes, a Git branch is a reference to a particular commit, and adding new commits moves the branch pointer forward, but forks off from the main (*master*) branch. In this way, they are lightweight and still connected to the entire history of the local repository:

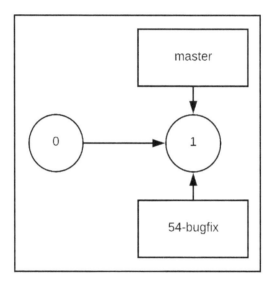

Once you've created a new branch, you still need to swap to it. This can be done with the powerful git checkout command. Specifying a branch name like git checkout 53-changing-font-colour will *check out* that branch from the repository, effectively swapping over your working directory and index to match the commit that was branched from. Any new commits you make will be applied to that branch, until you choose to git checkout another-branch.

If you want to create a new branch and swap to it immediately, you can use `git checkout -b branch-name-here` instead as a shortcut. `git checkout` also has the powerful ability to revert changed files and files that have been added to the staging index. If you run `git checkout — <filename>`, it will revert that file back to the status at the last point. Keep in mind that this will only work on files that have already been saved and committed to Git; new files can't be removed with this shortcut. This can save you a heap of time editing files back to their previous state.

If you've done some work and are happy with it, you may want to merge it back into the master branch of the code. You can do this with the aptly named `git merge` command. You swap to the branch you want to merge into, and then run `git merge branch-name-to-merge`. Let's say you have a situation like the following one:

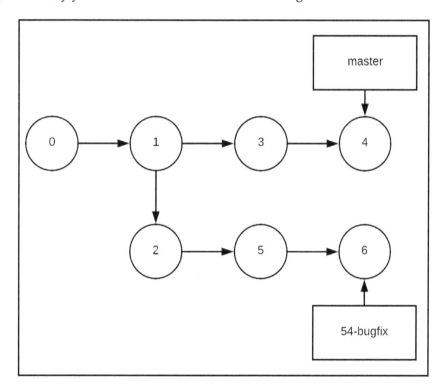

When you're on the master branch and run `git merge 54-bugfix`, behind the scenes, Git grabs those two commits and then finds their closest common ancestor:

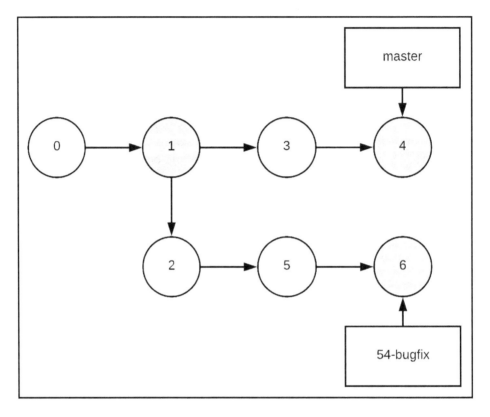

Git then attempts a three-way merge using the ancestor, the commit to be merged into, and the commit to merge in. This creates a new commit from all three, which your master branch is now pointing at:

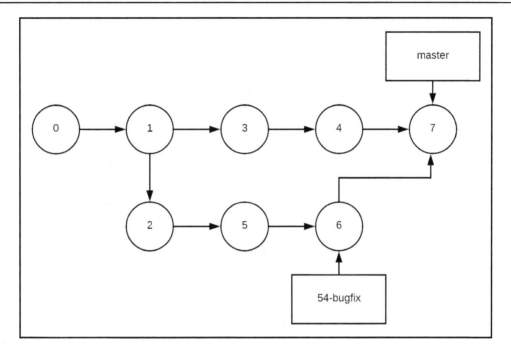

The `git status` command shows you the current state of changes in the working directory and index, showing you a list of what files are currently staged in the index and what files are in the working directory that differ from the previous commit. Running `git status` does a full update of the index, lodging any differences based on the modification times of the files.

The last command worth mentioning in this overview of git is `git diff`. `git diff` can be used by itself or you can append a file path (including wildcards) to show what has changed (the difference) between a file in the working copy and the last committed version. This can be useful for reviewing your changes before staging or committing them.

GitFlow

Git flow is a semi-standardized workflow for dealing with projects in Git. It can be daunting, but the rules involve creating a stringent practice for when branches should be committed to or merged in order to prevent deploying buggy code or releases. A diagram of it is as follows:

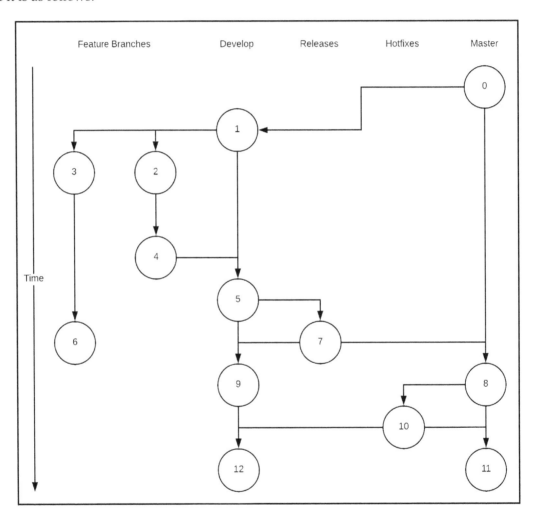

As you can see, there are a number of different *streams*. You have the master branch, hotfix branches for fixing emergency bugs, releases, the develop branch, and feature branches. These all have very particular uses, which we'll go into now.

Master

The master branch is the original branch where all code is branched from. However, it is never committed to directly; it is only ever merged into. The master branch is then used as the deployed branch, or the released branch if you have a product that is shipped. You can *tag* each merge with a version number to help identify these releases or deployed versions. It is worth reiterating here that code on the master branch should always be considered *production ready* and that no development should be occurring on this branch.

Develop

The develop branch is the other continuously existing branch in the Git flow model, along with the master branch. All other branches are considered temporary and can be deleted after work is finished on them and they've been merged.

This branch can often be the branch that the latest *nightly builds* are produced from and should have the latest delivered work available on it. Note that in many work environments, code will not be committed directly to the develop branch either, instead happening on feature branches that are then merged back in when the fix or feature is completed. Not all workflows are as strict, though, and some allow bug fixes or minor changes on the develop branch. However, this can be considered bad practice as it allows more bugs to be introduced into the main stream.

Most feature branches will be branched directly from develop, along with release branches as well, so it's good to keep this branch in a steady, known-good, and bug-free state.

Features

For each ticket that comes in, or for each project that is worked on, a feature branch can be created from the develop stream. Work is committed directly on this branch, and once in a sufficiently completed state, it can be merged back into develop. It's important to name these branches meaningfully; many teams tag these branches with references to the work/issue tracking system they use and sometimes with a meaningful name like `55-new-login-system`.

Unlike the develop or master branches, feature branches only need to last until the feature is complete and merged into develop, after which you can delete the branch since it should no longer be needed:

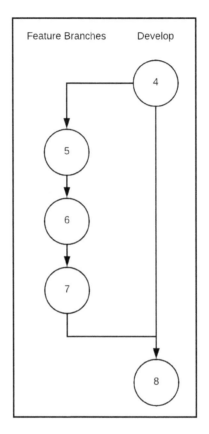

Releases

Release branches are a bit more complex than the ones that we have documented thus far. Release branches refer to an upcoming release and are branched from develop at a point where all work needed to be completed for a particular release is done. Commonly, the branch name will be prefixed with `release-` to help people know what the branch is for.

Once a release branch is created, no new features should be added to it. However, it's acceptable to add bug fixes as the extra testing used on these branches might uncover more problems. Each bug fix should be merged back into develop to ensure that develop gets the bug fix and prevent it from having to be fixed again down the line.

If everything is ready, the branch can be merged directly into the master and tagged appropriately as a new release (with either a major or minor version number, depending on your scheme). Once this is done, the branch should be re-merged into develop once more to ensure that all of the changes are back into the main development stream. You can then safely delete this branch since it is no longer required:

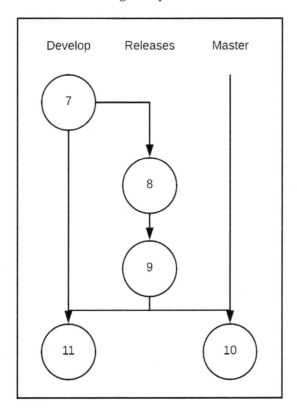

Hotfixes

Hotfixes are patches that are applied to critical bugs – these are mainly showstopping issues that are found in the master branch. In these cases, you make a branch from the master directly and usually prefix the branch name with `hofix-`, then make the fix on a new commit and merge back into master, tagging the master release with a new version (usually a minor or patch version, depending on your versioning strategy). After you've merged into master, you also need to merge this into develop so that develop has the latest patches and fixes and you don't conflict in future releases. The hotfix can then be safely deleted as it is no longer required:

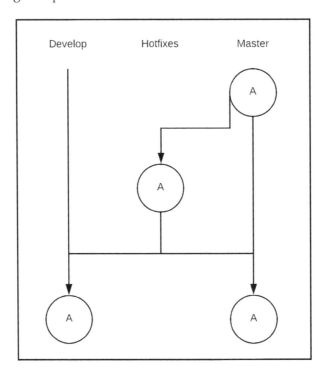

GitLab Flow

So far, we've explored GitFlow for collaborative project management, but it can be a complex one that doesn't suit all needs. There are alternatives, though, and one of these is posited by GitLab and thus known as GitLab Flow.

GitLab Flow is actually a collection of different branching strategies that can be used depending on your environments and needs. However, they all work on the basis that the master branch is the default branch to merge work into, rather than using a separate develop branch that not all software and CI/CD systems are set up to use by default.

Production branch

While some development environments can be deployed as soon as commits are merged in, some projects aren't set up like that. A good example is apps that need to be approved by the app store and thus aren't on the same agile, continuous release schedule as the code in the master branch, or platforms that can only be deployed during certain late night/early morning windows so as not to affect the users of the systems:

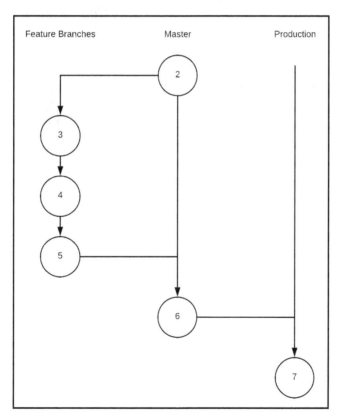

In this flow, you still have feature branches, but they are branched directly from the master and then merged directly back into the master once they have been completed. After each feature branch is re-merged, it can be safely closed. When you are ready for a deploy—let's say a few feature branches have been merged in and your weekly release is coming up – you simply create a merge commit into the production branch from the master and you have your code ready to go. Enterprising DevOps professionals can set up their continuous integration / continuous deployment systems to detect merges on the production branch and automatically deploy (or package and release) any code that is merged into it.

Staging branch

The production branch workflow is good, but sometimes you have multiple environments and your QA team might want to test stuff a bit further before it gets released. For example, you might have a staging or pre-production environment that you want to deploy to and ensure that everything is working before you deploy to production. In that case, you can use a workflow like the following:

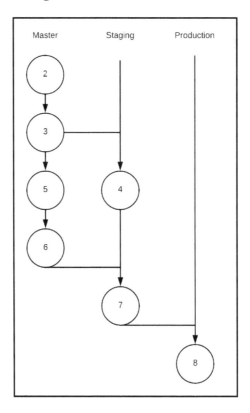

We've trimmed out the feature branches in the preceding diagram, but that part of the workflow would normally remain the same, rather than coding directly onto the master and risking conflicts and merge issues. However, you will notice that rather than merging directly from the master into our production environment, we merge into the staging environment instead. Commits are not done directly in staging either; instead, code must be merged into the master and only then merged back into staging and deployed to the staging environment. Once the release owners are satisfied with everything, a deploy can be made to the production environment by merging from staging into production.

Release branch

The last flow suggested by the GitLab team is the release branch flow. A handy diagram of it is included as follows:

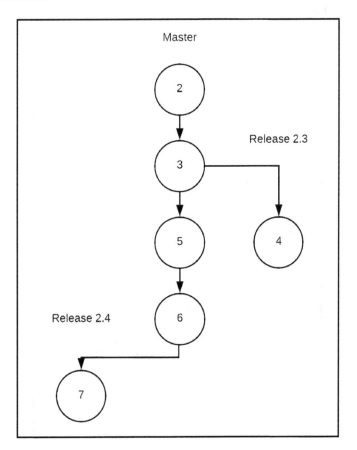

Once again, we haven't included the feature branches in the diagram, but they are still a key component of this workflow. Differently to the GitFlow, the feature branches merge directly back into the master branch rather than the develop branch. What are new, however, are the release branches, which are named after the release they represent. They are split directly from the master as they are completed. This is a useful branch if you release versioned software. Some people might want to keep access to older versions, or you may need to be able to recreate older versions for troubleshooting purposes or clients on older systems that aren't compatible with later releases.

Differences from GitHub flow

If you've previously worked with GitHub, you might be familiar with the GitHub flow, a rigid workflow which recommends only having a continuous master branch, from which features are branched off and then merged into when created. Any code in the master branch is theoretically ready for deployment and continuous release with the help of a CI/CD platform:

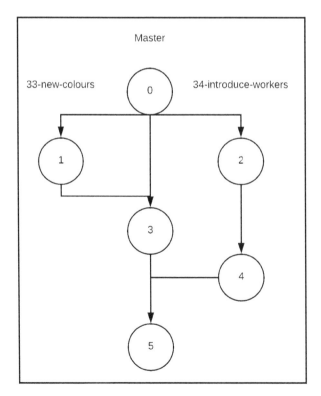

The main difference between the GitHub and GitLab flows is the flexibility of the latter. It provides blueprints for a number of different scenarios, each with slight differences in environment setup to cater to your project's needs. GitLab also avoids recommending the master for use in deployments, which can reduce the risk of bugs and ill effects being deployed.

Summary

In this chapter, we've looked at how to apply Git to your software development process and we've covered most of the basic commands, including add, commit, push, pull, branch, and merge. We also looked at GitFlow, a recommended workflow for Git software projects, and how to handle branching and merging correctly.

In contrast to the complexities of GitFlow, we also looked at GitLab flow, which is an alternate recommended flow that's been designed for simplicity and is adaptable to different environments.

In the next chapter, we'll look at using GitLab in our work, using issues to sort out items of work and performing merge requests to bring in changes that we've made.

4
Issues to Merge Requests

So far, we've been introduced to installing GitLab and have created a user for ourselves. We also familiarized ourselves with git commands and workflows, but how do we use GitLab? What are the essential parts of the platform that provide capability to us, aside from just being a place to host our code, which we in theory could do with a plain Git repository on any server.

Here's where we start tackling some more of the features of GitLab and how to work with it, so in this chapter, we'll look at the following topics:

- How to create a project in GitLab
- How to handle issues in GitLab
- How to handle merge requests in GitLab

Creating projects

To create a new project, follow these steps:

1. Direct your web browser to your GitLab URL. This will be either GitLab.com if you're using the SaaS version or the URL you specified when you installed GitLab on your server if you went with the self-hosted option.
2. Click the plus symbol (+) menu at the top.
3. Select **New Project.**
4. On this screen, fill out the details of your new project, as shown in following the screenshot.
5. Click **Create project**.

The project name should be descriptive and memorable, and the description should help explain what the project does. The **Visibility Level** changes project access to the levels it describes and is an important feature for creating private projects, limiting projects only to logged-in users (especially useful with limited registration or single sign-on), or allowing access from any public user if you want it visible to the world:

Once you've done this, you will be able to see the following screen. You'll notice that we haven't yet set up an SSH key; we'll lead you through this process shortly. If you scroll down a bit, you'll find some command-line instructions on getting yourself set up with the repository on your local machine. We'll lead you through some of these choices, as well as building our example project, before we move on to pulling in some issues for it:

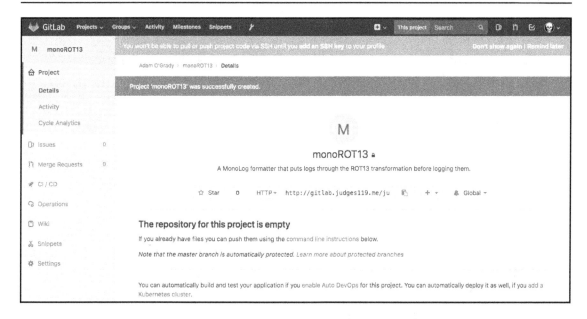

Creating an SSH key

To create an SSH key, follow these steps:

1. Click the profile icon in the top-right corner
2. Click the **settings** link
3. Select **SSH keys** from the left-hand side menu
4. Paste your SSH key in to the key section
5. Give your SSH key an informative and recognizable name
6. Click **Add Key**

On this page, there are also some links to tutorials on generating a new key or using an existing SSH key.

Committing to a project

Now that you've created your project and have an SSH key set up, we can start committing code to our project. First, let's make sure that we've configured our git client correctly. Run the following two commands to set your git username and email:

```
git config --global user.name "Biff Meerkat"
git config --global user.email "biff.meerkat@example.com"
```

Once you've done this, you can start working on your project. Depending on whether you've already started working or not, there's a couple of different ways to clone or prepare the repository.

Blank slate

If you're just starting out and haven't even created a new folder yet, you can clone the repository from GitLab and get started:

```
git clone git@gitlab.com:your_username/monoROT13.git
```

That's all you need to do and you'll be ready to go.

Existing folder

If you've already started working on your project but haven't yet created a git repository in your folder, you can run the following commands to get started:

```
cd existing_folder
git init
git remote add origin git@gitlab.com:your_username/monoROT13.git
```

Existing git repository

If you have an existing git repository and you want to add your GitLab repository as a remote repository and start committing, run the following commands:

```
cd existing_repo
git remote add origin git@gitlab.com:your_username/monoROT13.git
git push -u origin --all
git push -u origin --tags
```

Starting our example project

Our example project will be pretty simple: it will be a formatter for the PHP logging platform package Monolog. It will perform the ROT13 transformation on any logs passed to PHP, which turns any Latin alphabet character into the character 13 letters after it in the alphabet. Therefore, A becomes M, B becomes N, and so on.

Let's start by entering our project directory and creating a few folders. First, we'll create an src folder, and inside that a folder called Formatter. Now, we'll enter the Formatter folder and create a file called ROT13Formatter.php. Inside this file, add the following code:

```php
<?php
namespace Judges119\Monolog\Formatter;

use Monolog\Formatter\FormatterInterface;

class ROT13Formatter implements FormatterInterface
{
  public function format(array $record)
  {
    return str_rot13($record['message']);
  }

  public function formatBatch(array $records)
  {
    foreach ($records as $key => $record) {
      $records[$key] = $this->format($record);
    }
    return $records;
  }
}
```

Once you've done this, head back up to the project folder and run git add -A and git commit -m "Initial commit". You've successfully created your first commit, ready to be pushed to GitLab. You can now run git push origin master and the work will be pushed to your GitLab project.

Adding other project members

Once you've made some commits, you might want to add some project members. Open up your project, go to **settings**, and then go to **members** in the left menu. Here, you can invite new project members, set permissions for existing and new members, and remove members from a project. You can also set expiration dates for temporary members such as contractors, who might only be working on the project for a set time period:

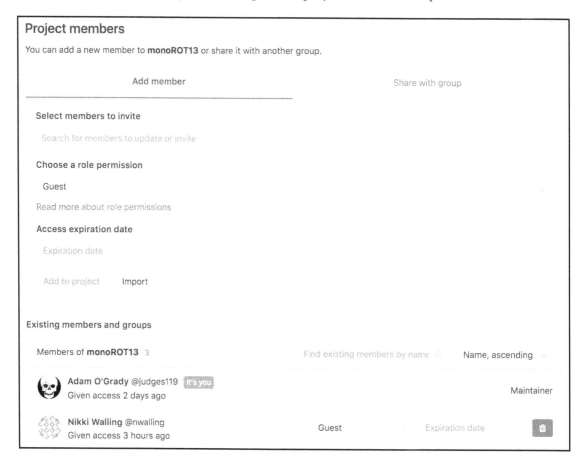

Now, let's visit our GitLab project web page and get started with handling issues.

Issues

From the main view of your project, select the **Issues** menu option on the left-hand side. Although the name typically refers to problems, it's here that you'll be doing a lot of the project management work, including setting up milestones, writing up feature requests, and divvying up work to different contributors. You should be faced with a screen that looks something like this:

The Issue Tracker is the place to add things that need to be improved or solved in a project

Issues can be bugs, tasks or ideas to be discussed. Also, issues are searchable and filterable.

New issue

Creating an issue

Click the **New Issue** button and you'll arrive at the **Create an issue** screen. This has a variety of fields that you can fill in to report on a problem or desired change in the GitLab project:

Let's fill out an issue. I think we should probably be using Composer (`https://getcomposer.org/`) to manage this PHP project, which is a perfect candidate for this. Click the **Assign to me** button as well so that we can get started on this issue shortly, and then hit **Submit issue**:

New Issue

Title	Composer

Add description templates to help your contributors communicate effectively!

Description

Write   Preview   B   *I*   ❞   ⟨⟩   ☰   ☷   ⊡   ⤢

You should probably include a composer.json so you can import modules properly and use this in other projects.

Markdown and quick actions are supported   🖻 Attach a file

◻ This issue is confidential and should only be visible to team members with at least Reporter access.

Assignee	Adam O'Grady	Due date	Select due date
Milestone	Milestone		
Labels	Labels		

Submit issue   Cancel

Something that's interesting to note is the ability to use GitHub-flavored Markdown to format your post. Markdown is a text markup language that allows you to simply add headings, bullet points, emphasis (bold or italics), numbered lists, and links or images in your text by using nothing more than some easily remembered symbols. We've included an overview of markdown syntax in the appendix:

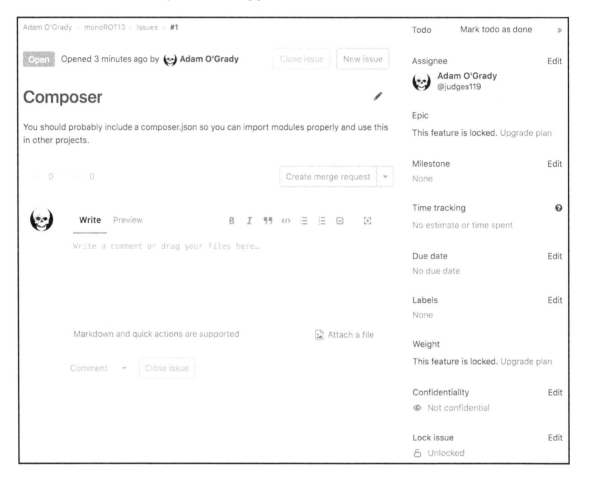

Now, you'll be able to see your issue, which will look something like the preceding screenshot.

Comments

You can add comments to an issue by filling out the comments box at the bottom. This is incredibly useful for starting a discussion on a problem. Much like in the description when creating an issue, you can use Markdown to format text. You can also tag other project members by typing the @ symbol and then their username, or selecting them from the drop-down list that appears. Typing a #, followed by an issue number (or searching in the drop-down box), lets you tag other issues in a comment too. Doing the same with a *!* or a *$* followed by a number will let you reference **Merge Requests** or **Snippets** as well:

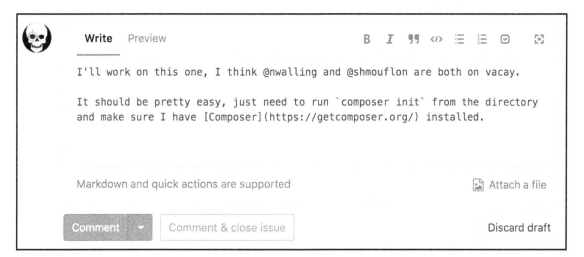

Once you submit the comment, you can see how it ends up being formatted:

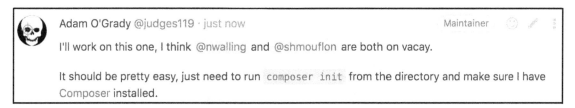

You'll also notice that you can add reactions to posts using the smiley face button in the top-right corner of a comment, or just following the issue (using either the same smiley face, or the up and down thumbs):

Unfortunately, you can't use the up or down votes on your own issue:

When authoring a comment, you can also select the drop-down arrow next to the **Comment** button and select **Start discussion**. This creates a specific topic of discussion within an issue that can be resolved and followed in one place:

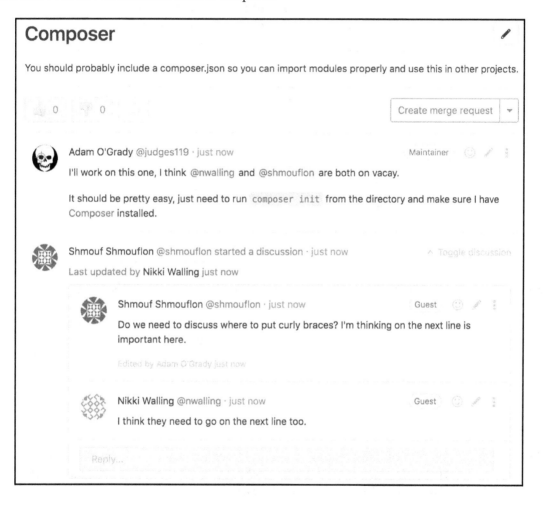

Issue board

The **Issue Board** is another big part of the GitLab workflow and can be heavily customized to suit your needs. You can reach the issue board for a project by going to the **Issues** option in the left-hand menu, and then **Board**. Here, you'll see a list of your issues:

For our project, we'll set up the default boards using the **Add default lists** button.

You can now click and drag issues between the boards to help indicate the progress on different issues. Let's start by moving the issue we created to **To Do** because we're going to get started on it soon. However, we need to investigate some other features of GitLab issues first.

Labels

Another important part of issue management and tracking is assigning labels to issues. If we click on **Labels** (under **Issues** on the left-hand side), we'll be taken to the labels screen. Here, we'll click **New label**, fill out a title and description, and pick a color:

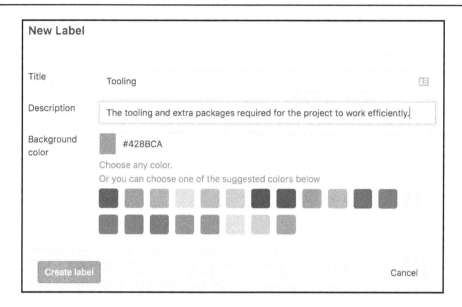

Now, we'll be back on the label board. You can click the star icon on a label to prioritize it, and then click and drag the prioritized labels up and down to prioritize them within that list:

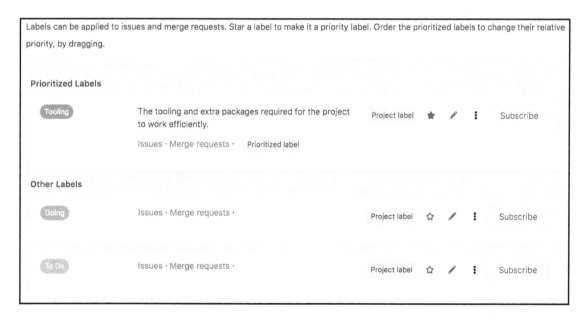

Let's go back to our issue (via **Issues** | **List or Issues** | **Board**) and then click to expand the sidebar on the right-hand side. Halfway down the list you should have **Labels**, with **To Do** already added. If you click **Edit** and then select **Tooling** and click the cross, you will now have another label assigned to the issue. This is a handy feature for managing a large numbers of issues. You can search for issues by labels on the **Issue List**, or go to the **Labels** section and click **Issues** on a label card be taken to a search for that label. This is useful if you want to track particular tasks, such as counting the number of tasks about documentation awaiting assignment, or looking at how much work is being dedicated to bug fixing compared to fulfilling feature requests.

Milestones

Milestones offer a way of grouping issues and merge requests that represent a specific release or timeboxed period to get work done. You can get to this section by clicking **Issues** and then **Milestones** in the left-hand side menu. Let's click on the **New Milestone** button on the left and then flesh one out:

After you've filled out all the fields, click the **Create milestone** button and you'll be taken to the board for that milestone. Now, you can assign issues to this milestone. Let's do this by going back to our issue (you can find it on the **Issue Board** or **Issue List**). On the right-hand side, you can expand the sidebar and click **Edit** next to **Milestone**. Select our new milestone from the list and you're done.

Now, if we go back to our milestone board, you will see our issue attached there:

Now that we've explored the basic functionality of issues, we can move on to updating our code and looking at merge requests.

Merge requests

Merge requests – commonly known as pull requests in other tools such as GitHub or BitBucket – are tasks that are assigned to someone that requests that they want to merge one branch into another. Using the GitLab flow described in `Chapter 3`, *GitLab Flow*, this is usually merging a feature branch into the master, or merging the master into a release, production, or pre-production/staging branch.

In this chapter, we'll continue using our example project to demonstrate the features of GitLab by creating a branch, completing some work, and then beginning a merge request. Next, we'll explore different parts of the merge request, including code review, assigning reviewers, and linking/closing issues from merge requests.

Example project continued

Let's continue with our example project by adding Composer integration. The GitLab flow policy says that we should be doing this work on a branch, and that branch names should start with the issue number followed by a hyphen-separated description of the branch. For our example, we'll use `1-add-composer.json` and check it out like so:

```
git branch 1-add-composer.json
git checkout 1-add-composer.json
```

We can also shorten this to the following:

```
git checkout -b 1-add-composer.json
```

Now, let's add our `composer.json` file. You'll need to follow the instructions to install Composer at `https://getcomposer.org`. Then, from the directory with your project, run the following:

```
composer init
```

This will lead you through an interactive prompt where you can specify a package name, author, license, and so on. Go through the prompt and choose not to interactively require dependencies or add to `.gitignore`.

We'll need to add some packages to our `composer.json` file as well, so run the following commands to add a dependency on Monolog:

```
composer require monolog/monolog
```

Now, we can commit the `composer.json` file and push it to the remote repository like so:

```
git add composer.json
git commit -m "#1 adding composer.json file"
git push origin 1-add-composer.json
```

Creating a merge request

If we go back to our issue view, we'll see that there's now a related branch:

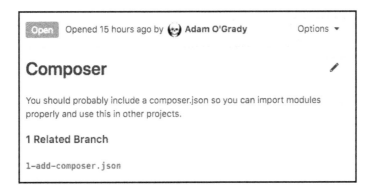

Let's click that branch name. We'll be taken to a view of the changed code. You'll see in this view that we can see the author of the commits and the changed files, including additions and deletions. Up at the top, you can also change the **Source** and **Target** if you wanted to compare different branches, such as merging a sub-feature into a feature branch, or the master into a staging branch:

Now, let's click the **Create merge request** button to get started on merging this code. You'll notice that the title and description have already been filled in with some information because GitLab has associated this branch with our issue. You can put `WIP:` at the start of the title of a merge request if you don't want it to be merged until you're ready. This indicates that the pull request is a **Work In Progress** and that you still have more commits to make before you're ready for review. This is commonly used on bigger changes when you might want someone to review your strategy or progress before you continue. If you put **Closes #54** or **Fixes #73**, GitLab will know that this merge request is associated with that issue and will close off that issue. Let's leave the issue request as it is and assign it to ourselves. You'll notice that you can also assign labels and/or milestones to a merge request, much like an issue. In this case, we'll assign the label and the milestone we created to this **merge request** (**MR**):

When you scroll further down, you'll see more fields that you can utilize. First, we have approvals, which is only available to paid plans but handy if you want to ensure that a merge request is approved by a specific person or people (potentially a domain expert, QA person, senior developer, and so on). You can also set a number of approvals that are required before merge – another feature that's useful for ensuring rigorous code quality standards by making a number of users review the code before merging. We also have the option to close the source branch on merge, which is handy for keeping the repository clean by deleting branches once they're complete. If you ever need to do more work on the branch, you can simply re-branch and commit work with no issues. Lastly, the option to squash commits before merging can be useful if you commit frequently but don't want to store the whole commit message history (especially if you have a tendency to name them `wip`, `wip2`, `more wip`, or `whoops bugfix`). This will simply squash all of the commits into one before doing the merge commit, and label the squashed commit with the title of the merge request:

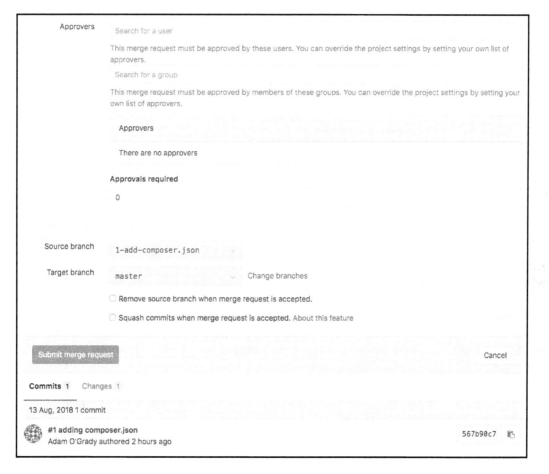

Let's click **Submit merge request** and move on to the next section: code review.

Code review with merge requests

You should now be faced with your merge request, which seems like a bit of a complex UI. Let's break down what we're seeing here:

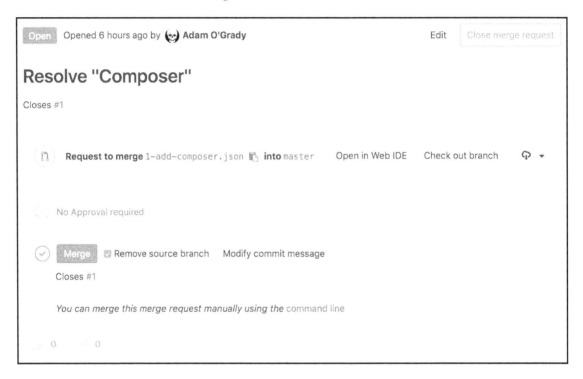

Across the top we have our status; some information about when it was created and by who; an **Edit** button if we want to change the title, description, approvals required, and so on; and a **Close merge request** button, which will decline the merge request immediately and close it. Not to worry though, you can reopen it again if you accidentally press this button. Next up, we have our title and description, which we can flesh out as much as needed. I've left it pretty sparse since this is just an example project, but you might want to put more information about the solution you used to solve the problem, how to test the code, and so on. After that, we have some information about the branch we are merging and merging into, with the option to inspect and edit the files in the web **integrated development environment** (IDE).

The button to **Check out branch** will open a modal with some instructions on how to check out and merge the branch locally, although merging locally isn't always possible if you have protected certain branches to stop them being committed to. The last button with the cloud/download icon presents a drop-down menu that allows you to download the patches as a plain git diff or an email patch.

The next part of the merge request deals with the approvals and merging. Approvals are a paid-only feature, so we won't be using them at the moment, but merging is definitely what we want to be doing. You have a chance to override the decisions to delete the source branch after you've completed it if you want to keep it for any reason, and also a button that lets you modify the merge commit message. The main showrunner here is the **Merge** button, which will automatically merge our work into the master branch. We won't click it for now, though, because there's a bit more to discover, such as the following:

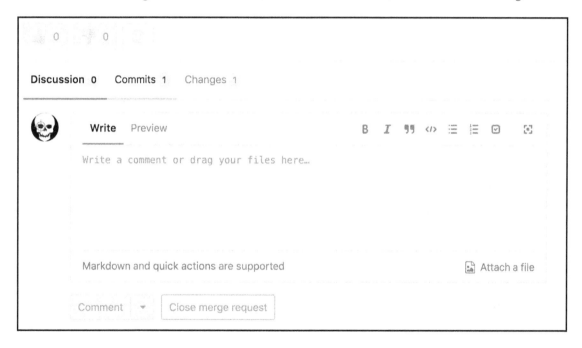

Just like with issues, you have the option to *react* to posts using a thumbs up or thumbs down, or an emoji reaction; however, remember that you can't react to your own MRs. We also have a discussion section where the merge request can be discussed. Make some comments now to try it out, and remember that there's a Markdown syntax guide in the appendix if you need some memory jogging. Like with issues, you can also use the dropdown to the right of the **Comment** button in order to **Start a discussion** in case you wanted to discuss something specifically, but have it nicely threaded and easily accessible and followable by anyone reading.

Now, click on the **Commits** tab next to the **Discussion** tab:

This is quite a simple view and just shows us the commits that make up our merge request. You can click a commit title to be taken directly to it if you want to see what changes it involved specifically, or copy the unique SHA hash, which identifies the commit using the clipboard symbol on the right. If you click the **Changes** tab next to the **Commits** tab, you'll be taken to the last main part of the merge request. Now, we can start auditing our code more directly:

```
Discussion 1    Commits 1    Changes 1

Showing 1 changed file ∨ with 15 additions and 0 deletions        Hide whitespace changes    Inline    Side-by-side

∨   composer.json 0 → 100644                              Edit    View file @ 567b90c7
     1  + {
     2  +     "name": "judges119/monorot13",
     3  +     "description": "A MonoLog formatter that puts logs through the ROT13 transformation
            before logging them.",
     4  +     "type": "library",
     5  +     "license": "BSD",
     6  +     "authors": [
     7  +         {
     8  +             "name": "Adam O'Grady",
     9  +             "email": "adam.ogrady@gmail.com"
    10  +         }
    11  +     ],
    12  +     "require": {
    13  +         "monolog/monolog": "^1.23"
    14  +     }
    15  + }
```

While this may just look like a normal diff window, it has one big difference. If you hover your mouse over the left-hand side, you'll see a little comment icon appear:

If we click that button, it opens up a comment window where we (or our colleagues) can comment on our code:

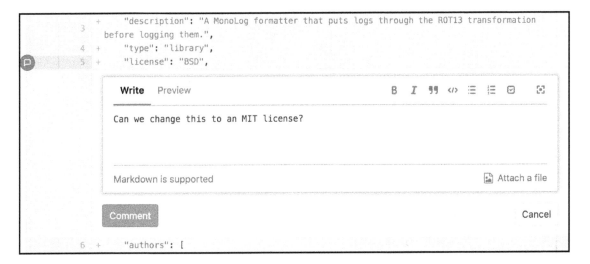

Here, we have our example comment. Now, we can hit the **Comment** button to finalize it:

Okay, it looks like my colleagues have a bit to say about my work already, and I've responded to one of them. Looks like we'll have some more work to do. I've also put a reaction on Shmouf's post using the smiley face icon and marked it as resolved using the little tick icon next to the commentor's role (the part that says **Guest**, **Maintainer**, and so on).

Now, open your `composer.json` file and change the license type to MIT, and then run the following:

```
git add composer.json
git commit -m "changing to MIT license"
git push origin 1-add-composer.json
```

Now, if you refresh your code review window, you'll see the changes and can mark the comment as resolved.

All that's left for us to do now is merge the commit using the **Merge** button that we discussed earlier. Once done, it'll change to show you that the merge has been completed, along with the merge commit hash:

If you've merged accidentally, you can *undo* the commit with the **Revert** button, which will have to create a new commit on the merged into branch. You can also **Cherry-pick** the code if you want to take this merge request and apply it to another branch.

Summary

By now, you should have a good handle on issues, merge requests, and working around GitLab. We've explored how to create new projects, why all new code should involve an issue and a merge request, how to apply labels and milestones, and how to review code with the GitLab user interface.

Now, we will move on to one of the bigger topics: continuous integration and continuous deployment. You can find out more about CI/CD, how GitLab does it, and how you can implement it in a project in the next chapter.

5
Continuous Integration and Continuous Deployment

Continuous integration and **continuous deployment**, commonly known as **CI/CD**, is a computing and IT philosophy whereby code is continuously tested and deployed/released automatically with as little manual handling as possible. This requires extra tools, usually a specialized platform that handles testing newly committed code as well as other tools that can take that code and package it for release, or upload it to a new version of the platform of website. However, if you're using GitLab, you have all the tools you need to get up and running and practicing CI/CD in no time.

In this chapter, we'll cover the following topics:

- How to install GitLab Runner
- Setting up tests in our GitLab example project
- The `.gitlab-ci.yml` file
- Setting up a `.gitlab-ci.yml` file in our GitLab example project
- Breaking down advanced `.gitlab-ci.yml` files
- The CI/CD interface in GitLab

By the end of this chapter, you'll have a good idea of how to navigate GitLab's CI/CD features and be ready to start integrating it into your own project.

How to install GitLab Runner

GitLab's implementation of a continuous integration and continuous deployment platform works off the idea of **Runners**, which are programs that are installed on other servers and can connect to the GitLab instance to receive jobs to run. These jobs can involve building, testing, and deploying code. In this section, we'll explore how to install GitLab Runner on Ubuntu, CentOS, and manually via binaries.

Ubuntu

To easily install GitLab Runner on Ubuntu, make sure that you have a recent version installed, as GitLab only provides packages for the currently supported versions. Next, open a Terminal session on your Ubuntu box and run the following command:

```
curl -L
https://packages.gitlab.com/install/repositories/runner/gitlab-runner/scrip
t.deb.sh | sudo bash
cat > /etc/apt/preferences.d/pin-gitlab-runner.pref <<EOF
Explanation: Prefer GitLab provided packages over the Debian native ones
Package: gitlab-runner
Pin: origin packages.gitlab.com
Pin-Priority: 1001
EOF
sudo apt-get install gitlab-runner
```

Let's break this down a bit.

The first command downloads and executes a script from GitLab that checks if your operating system is compatible, sets up your local package manager (`apt`) with the right URLs to get packages and lists from, and then updates those lists. This is a security anti-pattern, though, as the user isn't sure what they're executing and it could contain malicious code. I'd recommend downloading the script to your machine and then executing it yourself after having a read of the code so that you know what it will do.

The next section pins the package to the GitLab origin. This is necessary because Ubuntu introduced a GitLab Runner package as well. However, it can be a lot more out of date than the GitLab version and so it's recommended to pin it to the GitLab download origin.

Lastly, we install the package so that it's ready to go.

Now, we need to register the Runner. To do that, go to the *How to register Runners* section in this chapter.

CentOS

To easily install GitLab Runner on Ubuntu, make sure that you have a recent version installed, as GitLab only provides packages for the currently supported versions. Next, open a terminal session on your Ubuntu box and run the following command:

```
curl -L
https://packages.gitlab.com/install/repositories/runner/gitlab-runner/scrip
t.rpm.sh | sudo bash
sudo yum install gitlab-runner
```

Let's break this down a bit.

The first command downloads and executes a script from GitLab that checks if your operating system is compatible, sets up your local package manager (yum) with the right URLs to get packages and lists from, and then updates those lists. This is a security anti-pattern, though, as the user isn't sure what they're executing and it could contain malicious code. I'd recommend downloading the script to your machine and then executing it yourself after having a read of the code so that you know what it will do.

Lastly, we install the package so that it's ready to go.

Now, we need to register the Runner. To do that, go to the *How to register Runners* section in this chapter.

Binaries

If you don't want to use the DEB or RPM packages to install GitLab Runner, or are using an operating system without those package managers available, you can still install GitLab Runner manually using the binary downloads.

Run the following commands to download the Runner, give it permissions to execute, create a user for it, and then install and run it:

```
sudo wget -O /usr/local/bin/gitlab-runner
https://gitlab-runner-downloads.s3.amazonaws.com/latest/binaries/gitlab-run
ner-linux-amd64
sudo chmod +x /usr/local/bin/gitlab-runner
sudo useradd --comment 'GitLab Runner' --create-home gitlab-runner --shell
/bin/bash
sudo gitlab-runner install --user=gitlab-runner --working-
directory=/home/gitlab-runner
sudo gitlab-runner start
```

If you're using an ARM platform such as a Raspberry Pi or other lightweight device, you can change the `amd64` to `arm` in the download link.

How to register Runners

Once you have your Runner client installed, you can go through the process of registering it. There are two ways of doing this: in the administrator panel (only in self-hosted GitLab) or in project settings. The former creates a global **shared** Runner that can be assigned to multiple different projects or even made available to any project on the instance that needs a Runner. The latter method creates Runners that are tied specifically to a particular project/repository. There are also **group** runners, which can be assigned to a group of projects, but they are beyond the scope of this book.

Admin panel

To do this, you first need to log in to your GitLab instance as an account with administrator permissions. Once you're logged in, you need to click the spanner/wrench icon up the top at the end of the left-hand side menu. From here, go to **Overview** | **Runners** to be greeted by a scene like the following:

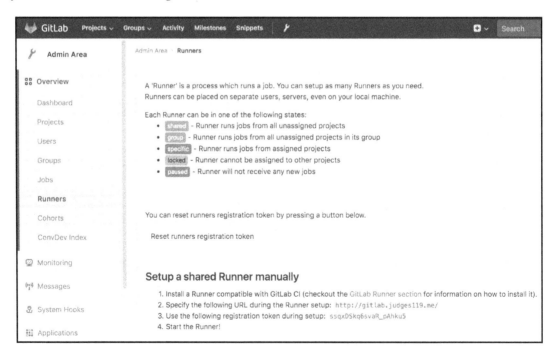

Finally, copy the value listed as the registration token, and move on to the next step.

Project settings

From your project home page, go to **Settings** | **CI/CD**. On this page, expand the section titled **Runners**. After the explanatory text, you'll be faced with an information box that looks like this:

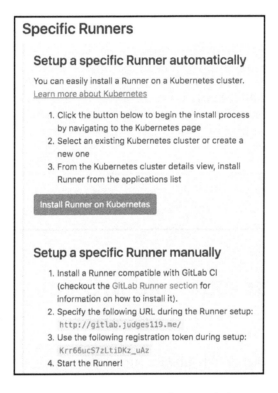

You'll need to copy the value for the registration token and then move on to the next step.

Registering the CLI

Jump into a terminal session on your GitLab Runner machine.

Run the following command:

```
sudo gitlab-runner register
```

This should lead you to an interactive prompt. First, you'll need to input the URL of your GitLab instance (make sure that it's reachable from the Runner). Next up, it will ask for the shared token that you copied earlier. Then, enter a name for the Runner and lastly a series of comma-separated tags. You can use these tags to describe or group the Runner, maybe by OS, capability, pre-installed frameworks, and so on. Lastly, you have to pick the GitLab Runner executor; this is how GitLab Runner will execute any tests. In most circumstances, you should select `docker`, but there are some occasions where you might want to select other options, such as `kubernetes` or `shell`. The latter is really helpful for building OS-specific projects, such as iOS apps that can't be easily built in a Docker container. If you do choose `docker` as your executor, you'll also be asked to provide a default Docker image for projects that do not specify one in their `.gitlab-ci.yml` file. You'll also need to make sure that Docker is installed on the Runner; it is not bundled with the Runner package.

Now, your runner should be ready to go. You can verify this in GitLab in the **Administration** | **Overview** | **Runners** or project home page by going to | **Settings** | **CI/CD** | **Runners**. For example, here's what it should look like if you set up a global runner in the administration panel:

Adding to our example project

To get started with testing, let's make an issue on our GitLab project and then create a branch, starting with the issue number.

In our example project, we'll need to update our `composer.json` file to look like the following:

```
{
    "name": "judges119/monorot13",
    "description": "A MonoLog formatter that puts logs through the ROT13
transformation before logging them.",
    "type": "library",
    "license": "BSD",
    "authors": [
        {
            "name": "Adam O'Grady",
            "email": "adam.ogrady@gmail.com"
        }
```

```
            ],
            "require": {
                "monolog/monolog": "^1.23"
            },
            "require-dev": {
                "phpunit/phpunit": "~4.5"
            },
            "autoload": {
                "psr-4": {
                    "Judges119\\Monolog\\": "src"
                }
            }
        }
    }
```

After you've done that, run the following command:

composer install

This will install the PHPUnit testing framework and set up the PSR-4 autoloading for our project. After you've run this, let's create a folder called tests and in that, a file called ROT13FormatterTest.php. In that file, put the following code:

```
<?php
require_once 'vendor/autoload.php';

use PHPUnit\Framework\TestCase;
use Judges119\Monolog\Formatter\ROT13Formatter;

final class ROT13FormatterTest extends TestCase
{

    public function testFormatReturnsString()
    {
        $formatter = new ROT13Formatter();
        $this->assertInternalType(
            'string',
            $formatter->format(["message" => "Changed to ROT13"])
        );
    }

    public function testROT13IsAccurate()
    {
        $formatter = new ROT13Formatter();
        $record = ['message' => 'ABC'];
        $transformed = $formatter->format($record);
        $this->assertEquals(
            $transformed,
            'NOP'
```

```php
            );
        }

    public function testROT13TextCanBeReversed()
    {
        $formatter = new ROT13Formatter();
        $record = ['message' => 'Changed to ROT13'];
        $transformed = $formatter->format($record);
        $transformed2 = $formatter->format(['message' => $transformed]);
        $this->assertEquals(
            $transformed2,
            $record['message']
        );
    }

    public function testFormatBatchReturnsArrayOfStrings()
    {
        $formatter = new ROT13Formatter();
        $records = [
            ['message' => 'Changed to ROT13'],
            ['message' => 'From ancient Rome'],
            ['message' => 'Modified Caesar cipher']
        ];
        $transformed = $formatter->formatBatch($records);
        $this->assertInternalType(
            'array',
            $transformed
        );
        $this->assertInternalType(
            'string',
            $transformed[0]
        );
    }
}
```

If you want to run the tests manually, you can change into your project directory in a terminal session and run the following command:

```
vendor/bin/phpunit tests/ROT13FormatterTest
```

You should see our tests pass, four for four. If your tests don't, you should examine the output of the logs to help you find and fix any errors. I'd recommend adding and committing the work you've done so far before we move on to learning about the `.gitlab-ci.yml` file.

Breaking down .gitlab-ci.yml

Continuous integration and continuous deployment in GitLab is described and defined by a project's `.gitlab-ci.yml` file. The file format is **YAML** (an acronym of **yet Another markup language**), which is a human-readable text file that's used for storing data, and can be converted into digital representations by a computer. This document is stored in the root directory of your repository and outlines all of the stages and work required for the CI/CD to run.

A basic `.gitlab-ci.yml` file might look something like this:

```
before_script:
  - apt-get update -qq && DEBIAN_FRONTEND=noninteractive apt-get install -y
-qq ca-certificates git php php-xml
  - php -r "copy('https://getcomposer.org/installer', 'composer-
setup.php');"
  - php composer-setup.php
  - php composer.phar install

phpunit:
  script:
    - vendor/bin/phpunit tests/ROT13FormatterTest
```

Because of the plain text format of YAML, along with the descriptive names, you can read the preceding code and have a rough idea of what happens. We can guess that `before_script` runs first, which runs a number of shell commands, followed by something called `phpunit`, which runs a script as well. However, we're still a bit in the dark about it all, so let's explore GitLab CI jobs, as well as some of the keywords.

Jobs

A *job* in `.gitlab-ci.yml` is a task or set of tasks that must be completed by a Runner. They are top-level entities within the `.gitlab-ci.yml` file, which are given an arbitrary name that's decided on by the author. It's a good practice to make the name descriptive to help summarize the purpose of jobs and make them easy to understand by others who might need to review or work with your CI/CD pipeline.

One thing that's important to note is that jobs are run independently of each other within the Runner, and thus different jobs can be picked up by different Runners. Jobs in the same stage (discussed as follows) can also be run in parallel on other Runners, allowing large pipelines to be broken down and completed faster than having to run everything in a sequential manner.

Under the job key/name, there are a number of different parameters/keywords that can be used to help define the job.

The script parameter

The most common parameter to a job, `script` is used to define any commands that should be run in the job. In our preceding example, we have the following:

```
phpunit:
  script:
    - vendor/bin/phpunit tests/ROT13FormatterTest
```

In the `phpunit` job, we have the `scripts` parameter, which tells GitLab to execute `vendor/bin/phpunit tests/ROT13FormatterTest`. It's worth noting that commands with special characters (such as a colon, brackets, ampersand, greater/less than, and so on) could be interpreted as part of the YAML, so it's prudent to wrap any such commands in single or double quotes to ensure that they are run as a command.

The before_script and after_script parameters

These are scripts that you choose to be run before the job is executed or after the job is executed. These can also be defined at the top level of the YAML file (where jobs are defined) and they'll apply to all jobs in the `.gitlab-ci.yml` file. `before_scripts` is executed before all jobs, including deploy tasks, but is run after artefacts have been restored (more on that shortly). `after_script` is run at the end of the job, even after failed jobs. This can be handy for cleaning up after a job has run.

The stage parameter

Stages are defined at the top level of the YAML file and are used to define separate blocks of jobs, which can be executed in parallel. They also define the order in which stages are run. In each job, the `stage` parameter can be used to define which build stage a job is in, thus grouping together similar jobs and allowing for jobs to depend on other jobs having finished. The following is an example of defining and using stages:

```
stages:
  - build
  - test
  - deploy

job 1:
```

```
    stage: build
    script: npm run build dependencies

  job 2:
    stage: build
    script: npm run build artifacts

  job 3:
    stage: test
    script: npm run test

  job 4:
    stage: deploy
    script: npm run deploy
```

In this case, we have defined three stages: `build`, `test`, and `deploy`. All of the jobs attached to the `build` stage can be run in parallel, and if they all succeed, the jobs with the `test` stage that have been identified will be run. Assuming they pass, the `deploy` jobs will then be run. If any job fails at an earlier stage, no further stages will be executed and the pipeline will be marked as failed.

The image parameter

The `image` parameter is used to specify which Docker image should be used when running a job. This can be specified as a parameter within a job, or at the top level to indicate a Docker image to be used by all jobs. Note that `image` parameters specified within each job will override the global `image` definition.

The services parameter

This parameter is used to specify extra Docker containers that can be connected to the test image to provision services. This is very handy for setting up databases to connect to, rather than needing to install your database engine on each build run. You can also specify this parameter in the top level (but it will be overriden by local definitions).

The only and except parameters

The `only` and `except` job parameters are used to limit when a specific job is run. `only` is used to limit a job being executed to a specified branch or tag names, while `except` is the opposite: the job will always be run unless it's on a specified branch or tag. The value for this parameter can be defined with a regular expression or a special keyword such as *branches* to refer to all branches, *tags* to refer to all tags, and so on. For more reserved keywords for `only` and `except`, please refer to the GitLab CI documentation online.

Please note that `only` and `except` don't have to be mutually exclusive either; you can use a combination of them to have more fine-grained control over when a job will be executed. An example of this is as follows:

```
job:
  only:
    - /^iss-.*$/
  except:
    - tags
```

In this case, the job will only be run on references where the label starts with `iss-`, and will not run on any tags that have been pushed to the repository.

There are more complex ways to use `only` and `except`, but they are beyond the scope of this quick start guide. More information can be found in the GitLab CI documentation (`https://docs.gitlab.com/ee/ci/`).

The tags parameter

You can specify a tag or tags in this parameter, which will limit this job to only being executed on Runners that also have the same tag. Please note that the tags are additive, so if you specify multiple tags, the job will only be executed on a Runner that has all of those tags present:

```
job:
  tags:
    - php
    - postgres
```

The preceding job will only be executed on Runners that have both the `php` and the `postgres` tag.

The allow_failure parameter

This parameter requires a Boolean response, either true or false. When false, the pipeline will execute as normal and any failures in that job will halt the rest of the pipeline. However, when set to true, that particular job can fail without stopping later tasks. The pipeline will still show green, but will have a *CI build passed with warnings* message displayed to alert users to the failed stage.

The when parameter

The when parameter can be one four values, and controls under which conditions a job is run. The possible values are as follows:

- on_success: The default behavior; a job will only be executed if the preceeding jobs/stages have passed
- on_failure: The job will only run if at least one job earlier in the pipeline has failed
- always: The task will always be executed, on both success and failures
- manual: A task that requires manual intervention to be started, such as from the GitLab web UI

One example use case of when is as follows:

```
stages:
  - build
  - cleanup_build

build_job:
  stage: build
  script:
    - webpack

cleanup_build_job:
  stage: cleanup_build
  script:
    - rm /dist/*
  when: on_failure
```

In the preceding case, the build job is always executed and attempts to use webpack to build our JavaScript assets, but if it fails, the cleanup_build_job task will be run, deleting any files that were created by the former task.

The environment parameter

The environment parameter is used to specify a particular environment to which a job will be deployed. Environments are discussed in the *Environments* section later in this chapter. The environment key can contain multiple other keys, most commonly `name` and `url`. The `name` sub-key defines a name for an environment to which the code will be deployed. You can track this using the GitLab web user interface by going to **Project** | **Operations** | **Environments**. While you can create new environments in the web user interface, it's recommended that you define them first in the `.gitlab-ci.yml` file, which will automatically create them in the web UI on its first run. The `url` parameter will be exposed in multiple parts of the GitLab web user interface as links and buttons that can be used to access the environment.

The cache parameter

To speed up build processes, you can cache certain files and directories between jobs and between different pipeline executions using the `cache` keyword. This is a more advanced strategy, but is really useful to reduce turnaround time in your CI/CD pipelines if you want builds to be tested, packaged, or deployed rapidly. The `cache` parameter can take a few different parameters itself to help define the caching rules. Please note that caching can be defined locally (per-job) or globally, and that local caches will override any global declarations.

To manually clear caches, you can open the GitLab web user interface for your project and navigate to **CI/CD** | **Pipelines** using the menus on the left. From here, click the **Clear Runner Caches** button.

cache – paths

This is an array of paths to files and/or directories that should be cached. You can also use the asterisk wildcard character (*). This is demonstrated in the following code snippet:

```
build:
  cache:
  paths:
    - binaries/*.apk
    - .config
```

In the preceding example, we cache the `.config` file as well as any `.apk` files in the `binaries` directory.

cache – key

This takes a string that can be used to create separate caches for different jobs or branches, like so:

```
test:
  cache:
    key: "$CI_COMMIT_REF_SLUG"
    paths:
      - binaries/
```

In this example, we use an inbuilt default variable provided by GitLab CI – `CI_COMMIT_REF_SLUG` – that is equal to the branch/tag name of the commit. In this case, GitLab CI will maintain a separate cache for each branch. Next up, let's look at jobs with different paths cached:

```
stages:
  - build
  - test

build_job:
  stage: build
  script: npm run build
  cache:
    key: build-key
    paths:
      - public/

test_job:
  stage: test
  script: npm run test
  cache:
    key: test-key
    paths:
      - vendor/
```

Without a `key` value, this would mean that the second job to run (`test_job`) would reuse the cache from `build_job` and at the end of its run would cache the `vendor/` directory. This cache will overwrite the existing cache from `build_job`, which means that next time the pipeline runs, the cache will only contain the `vendor/` directory (as that was the only thing defined to be cached by the last running job) and the cache will be useless to `build_job`. To prevent this happening, we use a separate cache key, which means that each time the pipeline is run, `build_job` will grab the cache stored under the `build-key` value and `test_job` will use the cache stored under `test-key`.

cache – untracked

This is a simple helper option that you can set to `true` in order to cache any files that are untracked by git at the end of a job run. This is handy for caching the output left over from package installations or program compilation.

cache – policy

Under default circumstances, the cache is downloaded before every job and then re-uploaded at the end of the job. This is equivalent to setting the following:

```
job:
  cache:
    policy: push-pull
```

You may have a pipeline with jobs that would use a cache but not alter the contents of the cache. A good example is having one job that downloads all of the required packages and builds assets, and then subsequent jobs that simply run tests. In these cases, you can set `policy: pull`, which will download the cache at the start of the job but skip the uploading phase to save time. Conversely, if you have a job that always creates the contents of a cache, you can set `policy: push`, which will skip the download phase but always run the upload step at the end of the job.

The artifacts parameter

The `artifacts` parameter is used to define a list of files and directories that should be attached to a job after success. They are packaged and sent to the GitLab instance (either your self-hosted one or GitLab.com) and become available for download through the web user interface.

artifacts – paths

Much like with caching, you specify an array of paths, which can include wildcards like so:

```
package:
  artifacts:
    paths:
      - public/
      - tests/*.html
```

In this case, everything in the `public/` directory as well as any HTML files in the `tests/` directory will be zipped, uploaded, and made available for download in the web user interface.

artifacts – name

By default, any uploaded files will be stored in a `.zip` archive titled `artifacts.zip`. You can use the `name` parameter to change the default filename (it will still end with `.zip`), as demonstrated in the following code:

```
package:
  artifacts:
    name: cool_project_name
```

In the preceding example, every time this job is completed, a zipped file called `cool_project_name.zip` will be uploaded to GitLab and made available for download in the web UI. However, this is not the limit of the naming parameter. You can use built-in GitLab variables such as `CI_JOB_NAME` (the name of the currently running GitLab CI job) or `CI_COMMIT_REF_NAME` (the name of the branch/tag) to create dynamically named artifacts like in this example:

```
package:
  artifacts:
    name: "$CI_JOB_NAME-$CI_COMMIT_REF_NAME"
```

The preceding example will label every artifact with the current job name (in this case, `package`) and the current git branch name, separated by a hyphen and followed by `.zip`.

artifacts – untracked

Much like the `untracked` key in the `cache` section, `artifacts:untracked` is a boolean variable that can be set to `true` in order to collect all untracked files and upload them as artifacts.

artifacts – when

The `when` key can have one of three different values and controls under what circumstances artifacts are uploaded:

- `on_success`: Only upload artifacts when the job is successful (default).
- `on_failure`: Only upload artifacts when the job fails. This is useful if you want to examine failed builds.
- `always`: Upload artifacts, regardless of whether the job succeeds or not.

artifacts – expire_in

The `expire_in` sub-parameter is provided with a string defining how long artifacts should be kept for in the GitLab instance. If this is not specified, it defaults to the instance setting, which is 30 days by default for self-hosted GitLab or forever for GitLab.com projects. Some examples of strings that you can provide include the following:

- 42 weeks
- 42 days
- 42 mins 42 secs
- 2 mos 1 day
- 42 years 6 mos 6 hrs
- 1 week and 2 days

Keep in mind that the job that deletes old artifacts is run on an hourly basis, so units of time less than one hour might not be effective. There is also a **Keep** button in the GitLab web user interface that can be used to keep an artifact forever and override the specified time value.

The variables parameter

You can store variables per job or globally using the `variables` keyword. The value for `variables` should be an array of key/value pairs that can be represented by strings or integers (for both key and value), although typically the key will be an all-capitalized string for ease of recognition. Any variables used should be of a non-sensitive nature; they are not considered an appropriate method for storing secrets. Locally defined variables will override their globally defined counterparts, but to have a job run with no access to globally defined variables, you should redeclare it with an empty array like so:

```
cool_job_name:
  variables: {}
```

Other parameters

So far, we've covered the majority of the parameters that are available to jobs, including a bunch of ones that can be used at the top level to apply to all jobs. It's worth noting that there are other ones such as dependencies, coverage, and so on that are beyond the scope of this book, but can be found in the GitLab CI documentation online. Let's move on to creating a `.gitlab-ci.yml` file for our project so that we can start testing our commits.

Adding .gitlab-ci.yml to our example project

We've added tests to our `ROT13Formatter` project, but now we need to get those tests to be automatically executed in GitLab (either `GitLab.com` or our own hosted instance). To do this, let's create a file called `.gitlab-ci.yml` in our project and add the following to it:

```
before_script:
  - apt-get update -qq && DEBIAN_FRONTEND=noninteractive apt-get install -y
-qq ca-certificates git php php-xml
  - php -r "copy('https://getcomposer.org/installer', 'composer-
setup.php');"
  - php composer-setup.php
  - php composer.phar install

phpunit:
  script:
    - vendor/bin/phpunit tests/ROT13FormatterTest
```

This exact file was discussed in the previous section, so we know that it simply executes a series of commands to configure the Runner and then runs one task that executes our tests. Now save, commit, and push this file to GitLab, and then we'll almost be ready to have our pipeline running. If you've set up a shared Runner in GitLab (as discussed earlier in this chapter), you'll need to go to **Admin Area** | **Overview** | **Runners**. From here, edit your Runner and tick **Run untagged jobs**; this will allow your Runner to pick up jobs that don't have tags (which our new .gitlab-ci.yml file lacks):

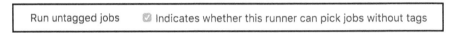

Now, when you go to **Project** | **CI/CD** | **Pipelines**, you should see your new pipeline there, ready to go:

The status may also be **running** if the pipeline is still processing, **pending** if you have no free Runners, or **failed** if the pipeline failed somewhere along the pipeline.

You can click the status (**passed**, in the preceding screenshot) to receive a breakdown of the pipeline. Yours should look similar to this:

The commit name and branch might be different, but the main area under the **Pipeline** heading should look the same. It's pretty bare, but that's only because we have a single stage in our CI/CD pipeline, and within that stage we have a single task, `phpunit`. In more complex pipelines, you'll have multiple different stages shown, and each stage might have many different jobs within it.

You can click the **Jobs** heading to view the status of the individual jobs within the pipeline. This view will be pretty bare because we have such a simple pipeline, but you should still see the status, job ID, and name. By clicking on the status, you'll be taken to that individual job, which will show the current progress of it. The following is an example from an in-progress job execution:

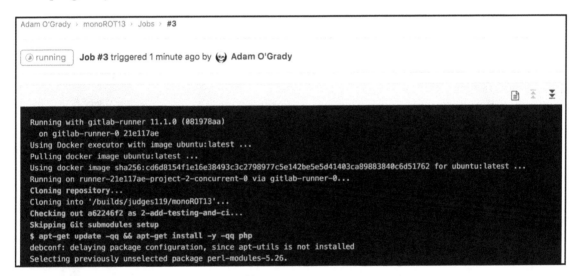

As you can see, we have the job status and some information, followed by a large block of text indicating the output from any scripts being executed in the course of the job.

Deconstructing an advanced .gitlab-ci.yml file

Now that we've configured GitLab to run continuous integration and continuous deployment with our example project, it's worth exploring a more advanced `.gitlab-ci.yml` file and breaking it down to make sure that we understand what all of the components do. To this end, here's an example file that uses more jobs and more advanced parameters:

```yaml
image: bitnami/laravel:latest

services:
  - postgres:9.6

variables:
  POSTGRES_DATABASE: postgres
  POSTGRES_PASSWORD: password
  DB_HOST: postgres
  DB_USERNAME: root

stages:
  - test
  - package
  - deploy

php_unit_test:
  stage: test
  script:
    - cp .env.example .env
    - composer install
    - php artisan key:generate
    - php artisan migrate
    - vendor/bin/phpunit
  cache:
    key: composer
    paths:
      - vendor/

js_unit_test:
  stage: test
  script:
    - npm install
    - npm run test

package_upload:
  stage: package
```

```
script:
  - composer install
  - npm install
  - webpack
cache:
  key: composer
  paths:
    -vendor/
  policy: pull
artifacts:
  paths:
    - public/
  expire_in: 1 week
  only:
    - tags

deploy_production:
  stage: deploy
  script:
    - composer install
    - npm install
    - webpack
    - .composer/vendor/bin/envoy run deploy
  environment:
    name: production
    url: http://192.168.0.1
  when: manual
  only:
    - master
```

Let's break some parts of this down:

1. The header of the `.gitlab-ci.yml` file defines an image to use from the Docker Registry (`image: bitnami/laravel:latest`), as well as defining a `service` (in this case, the `postgres:9.6` image, also from the Docker registry). This service container will be attached directly to our Laravel image to provide a database without needing to set up a database as part of a `before_script` each time a job is run:

   ```
   image: bitnami/laravel:latest
   services:
     - postgres:9.6
   ```

2. The variables that are declared all relate to our database and will be used in the jobs so that we can connect to our database service image. Of particular note is the DB_HOST parameter, which simply specifies postgres as the hostname. This is because with GitLab CI, any services that are connected are referred to by their image name, in this case, postgres:

```
variables:
  POSTGRES_DATABASE: postgres
  POSTGRES_PASSWORD: password
  DB_HOST: postgres
  DB_USERNAME: root
```

3. Next, we define three stages that we want: test, package, and deploy. These stages will be run sequentially (and any errors in an earlier stage will cause the whole pipeline to be canceled):

```
stages:
  - test
  - package
  - deploy
```

4. During the test stage, we'll have two separate jobs that can be run simultaneously (provided there are enough available Runners). php_unit_test and js_unit_test don't depend on one another, so they can safely be run together without causing problems. Both jobs are quite similar in that they have mostly the same parameters, although their scripts each perform very different functions. The big difference between the two is that php_unit_test also contains a cache section, which means that after the job is finished, the entire vendor/ directory will be zipped up and stored under the composer key for reuse in future jobs and pipelines. This helps reduce the time taken to build and execute subsequent runs of this job and any other jobs that use the same cache. Once both jobs are finished (and both are successful), the next stage can begin:

```
php_unit_test:
  stage: test
  script:
    - cp .env.example .env
    - composer install
    - php artisan key:generate
    - php artisan migrate
    - vendor/bin/phpunit
  cache:
    key: composer
    paths:
      - vendor/
```

```
js_unit_test:
  stage: test
  script:
    - npm install
    - npm run test
```

5. The `package_upload` job is the only component of the `package` stage, and consists of a script that installs all of the required dependencies and compiles all the front-nd elements. To speed up this process, we use the `cache` key, which should download the cache used in the earlier `php_unit_test` if it's available. For this example, we've also set the `policy` to `pull` to demonstrate it. This means that while it will download any available cache stored under the `composer` key, it will not re-upload any files once the job has finished. This task will also only operate on tagged commits, which is handy if you're doing versioned releases of software. Once all of the scripts have been executed, all of the files in the `public/` directory will be packaged and uploaded as artifacts and stored for up to a week:

```
package_upload:
  stage: package
  script:
    - composer install
    - npm install
    - webpack
  cache:
    key: composer
    paths:
      -vendor/
    policy: pull
  artifacts:
    paths:
      - public/
    expire_in: 1 week
    only:
      - tags
```

6. The last stage to run is `deploy_production`, which will only be available if the preceding stages have completed successfully. Note that if a job (such as `package_upload`) doesn't run because it isn't a tagged release, the stage can still be considered to have run successfully. The `deploy_production` task will run a script that installs all of the dependencies and prepare any necessary files and then deploy itself (the last command in the `script` array). Given that we are provided with a name and a URL under the `environment` parameter, you can find the status of the deployment in the GitLab web user interface for the project under **Operations** | **Environments**, and then under the name provided (`production`). There will also be links to the deployed application in the project user interface so that you can inspect it once it's live. Please note that this job will only run when code is pushed to the master branch:

```
deploy_production:
  stage: deploy
  script:
    - composer install
    - npm install
    - webpack
    - .composer/vendor/bin/envoy run deploy
  environment:
    name: production
    url: http://192.168.0.1
  when: manual
  only:
    - master
```

GitLab CI/CD web UI

While we've explored how to get GitLab CI up and running by creating a `.gitlab-ci.yml` file and looked at many of the configuration options available, we've only taken a brief look at the GitLab web user interface for continuous integration and continuous deployment. Let's break down the GitLab web user interface and look at how we can manage and inspect pipelines, jobs, charts, environments, and other common tasks.

The pipelines screen can be accessed under your project by going to **CI/CD** and then
Pipelines through the left-hand side menu. You should then be faced with a screen that
looks something like the following:

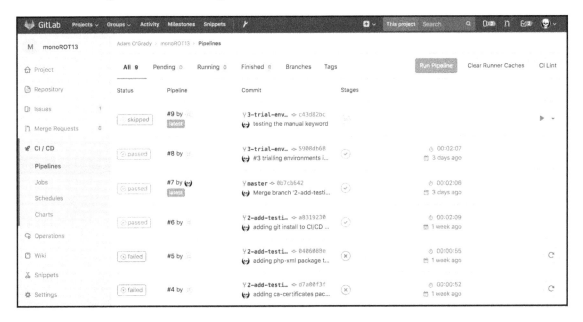

Here, you can view a list of the pipelines that have run or are currently running, as well as
their status (failed, passed, skipped, and so on), who organized them, what branches and
commits they are for (including the commit message), the success/failure of each stage
(represented by the tick boxes), and the runtime and when it completed. You'll notice
across the top left that there are also some buttons that provide extra functionality. You can
click **Run Pipeline** to organize a manual, immediate run of the pipeline against a preferred
branch. There's also the aforementioned **Clear Runner Caches** button, which will
immediately clear the cache on all connected Runners. The last button, **CI Lint**, takes you to
a small web application that can be used to lint a `.gitlab-ci.yml` file to ensure that the
syntax is correct.

The output of a linted `.gitlab-ci.yml` file looks like this:

Check your .gitlab-ci.yml

Content of .gitlab-ci.yml

```
 1   image: bitnami/laravel:latest
 2
 3 ▾ services:
 4     - postgres:9.6
 5
 6 ▾ variables:
 7     POSTGRES_DATABASE: postgres
 8     POSTGRES_PASSWORD: password
 9     DB_HOST: postgres
10     DB_USERNAME: root
11
12 ▾ stages:
13     - test
14     - package
15     - deploy
16
17 ▾ php_unit_test:
18     stage: test
19 ▾   script:
20       - cp .env.example .env
21       - composer install
22       - php artisan key:generate
23       - php artisan migrate
24       - vendor/bin/phpunit
25 ▾   cache:
```

Validate   Clear

Status: syntax is correct

If the syntax passes its validation, you'll be shown the preceding message, as well as a table (visible in the following screenshot) that breaks down the keys and values provided in the script. You can use these to sanity check your work:

Parameter	Value

	`cp .env.example .env`
	`composer install`
	`php artisan key:generate`
	`php artisan migrate`
	`vendor/bin/phpunit`

Test Job - php_unit_test	**Tag list:** **Only policy:** **Except policy:** **Environment:** **When:** on_success
	`npm install` `npm run test`
Test Job - js_unit_test	**Tag list:** **Only policy:** **Except policy:** **Environment:** **When:** on_success

From the left menu under **CI/CD**, you can click **Jobs** to get a listing of all of the running, failed, and succeeded jobs. This view (shown in the following screenshot) provides information about each job, including the following:

- Status
- Branch
- Commit
- Pipeline

- Stage
- Name
- Run time
- Finish time

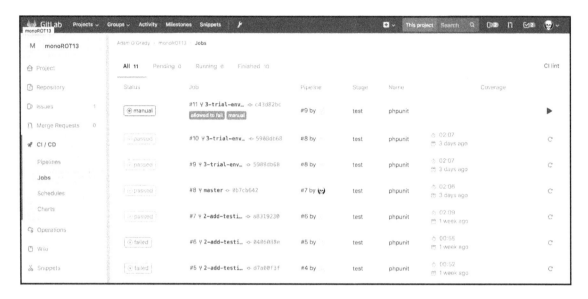

Looking at the preceding screenshot, you'll will be able to see a play button that can be clicked to initiate a job that requires manual involvement. Completed jobs also have a **Re-Run** button, which can be used to run the job again. Please note that these buttons are only available to people with the proper permissions in the GitLab instance. If there are artifacts to be downloaded, you'll also see a download button, which can be clicked on to begin downloading the zipped file containing all of the artifacts that were built in that job. If you only want to view the jobs relating to a specific pipeline, from the pipelines screen you can click the status of a pipeline and then click the **Jobs** tab to find similar information. However, this is limited to jobs that have been attached to that pipeline run.

From the menu on the left, under **CI/CD**, you can click **Charts** to get some graphical information about the CI/CD process attached to this project:

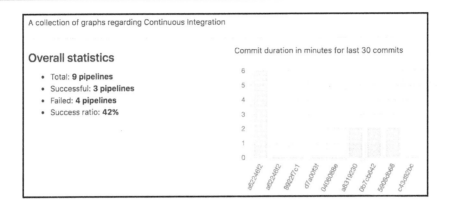

The first section contains some data breakdowns next to a chart of the times required for the pipelines to run. This can be useful for diagnosing issues with your pipelines and analyzing when pipelines need to be optimized to reduce time-to-completion and speed up the development/test/release life cycle. Next up, we have charts showing the breakdown of pipelines over the past week, month, and year:

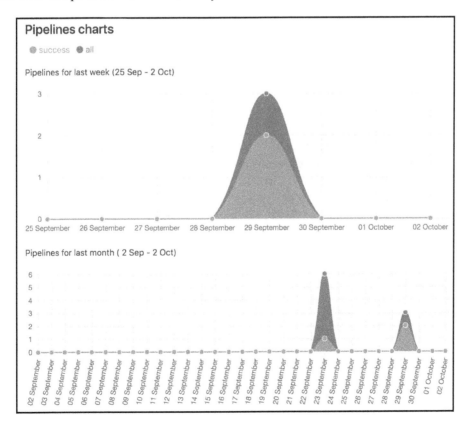

You can see that it outlines both the total pipelines and the subset of successful pipelines in the charts. This can give good metrics on the active times for a project, as well as show trends relating to work that has been completed.

The last section of interest to us is **Environments**. By clicking on **Operations** | **Environments** through the menu on the left ,you'll be faced with a screen that looks similar to the following:

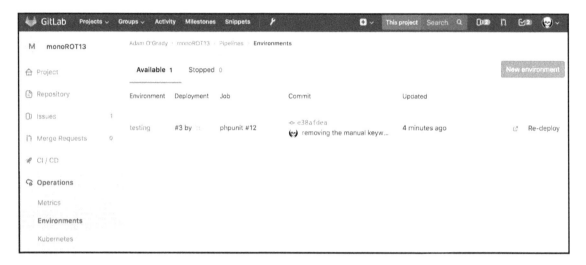

This shows all of the environments that your app has been deployed to which have been defined in your `.gitlab-ci.yml` file. It shows the name of the environment, the deployment and job that deployed to it, as well as the particular commit that has been loaded on it. Next up is the last updated time, followed by two important buttons. The first one links directly to the environment (opening it in a new tab) and is only available if you specified a URL parameter when defining an environment in your `.gitlab-ci.yml` file. The last button allows you to redo the deployment process in case anything went awry the first time.

Summary

By now, you should have a firm grip on the basics of continuous integration and continuous delivery, as done by GitLab. We started out in this chapter by exploring the concept of CI/CD and giving you a crash course in it.

Next up, we ran through the process of installing a GitLab Runner. Don't forget that the Runner is the platform where your CI/CD stages are actually executed; you can have many of them per project or per GitLab installation to help parallelize the work. We looked at their installation on Ubuntu and CentOS, and manually installing one via a binary. This was followed up by configuring the Runner in the GitLab web UI and then registering it on the Runner host so that it knew which GitLab URL to connect to and set up the registration token it would need.

After we finished configuring Runners, we updated our sample project with some tests to give it a reason to need a CI/CD platform. This was followed by a dive into the required `.gitlab-ci.yml` file, which outlines how the pipelines work for your project. We looked at jobs and a lot of the parameters you can supply to properly configure jobs in GitLab CI. We then set up our own `.gitlab-ci.yml` file for use with our sample project and pushed it to GitLab. From here, we investigated some of the web UIs for GitLab's CI/CD to help familiarize the user with how they can keep an eye on their projects.

In the next chapter, we'll look at porting your projects from GitHub and other Git hosting platforms, as well as moving over from other version control systems such as Subversion.

6
Porting from GitHub or Subversion (SVN)

So far, we've explored GitLab as a code hosting platform and looked at creating new projects on it. While this is perfect if you're starting out with GitLab in your organization, you may have an existing code-hosting platform, or even use a different version control system for your projects, and are looking at moving to GitLab.

Thankfully, GitLab has recognized this as a barrier to people moving over, and provides a number of easy methods for moving your projects to it as a code-hosting and testing platform. In this chapter, we'll look at the following:

- Moving to GitLab from GitHub, and more
- Moving to GitLab from a Git repository
- Moving from Subversion (SVN) to GitLab

Changing code-hosting platform

Many organizations, and even just established personal projects, already have a preferred code-hosting platform. There are a lot on the market and they all have benefits and drawbacks that can lead to them being chosen. However, times change and sometimes business or project needs can force a move to a different platform. We'll now look at some common reasons that your organization might have for changing their code-hosting platform:

- **Cost**: `GitLab.com` is free to use; paid accounts only unlock extra features. You can also host a GitLab instance on your existing hardware.
- **Data sovereignty**: You can host your own GitLab instance on your own hardware and be in control of your data.
- **Trust and transparency**: GitLab is free and open source software (FOSS); you can examine the code that runs on your instance or GitLab.com, and be certain that it's free of nasties.
- **Features**: Many code-hosting platforms are simply places to host your code. GitLab provides a whole continuous integration/continuous deployment suite as well as tools to help you monitor your production environment or host the outputs from your build process for public download.
- **End-of-life**: Nothing lasts forever and your existing code-hosting platform may be shutting down, so moving to another platform is recommended before you lose everything.
- **No one examined the competition**: Maybe someone originally picked one they knew without considering the benefits and disadvantages of the competition, and now it's time to check out the playing field.

Let's take a look at a few of the common platforms for code hosting and demonstrate how to move from them to GitLab.

GitHub

One of the biggest names in code hosting, GitHub is probably the most well-known place to store your code. If you want to move from GitLab to GitHub, thankfully there's an easy way to do it:

1. From the main screen, click the + icon up at the top and then select **New Project**. On this page, select the **Import project** tab:

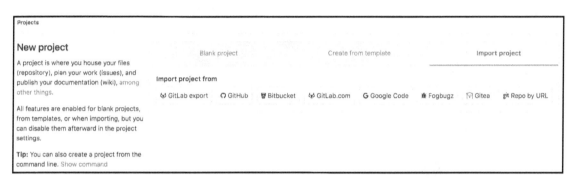

2. Click the **GitHub** button and you'll be taken to the **Import repositories from GitHub** page. The content on this page will differ depending on whether you're using your own GitLab instance (and haven't enabled the GitHub integration) or if you're using an instance integrated with GitHub, such as GitLab. Enabling GitHub integration is outside the scope of this chapter but GitLab online administration documentation can walk you through it if you desire. If you don't have GitLab integration, you'll still have the option of importing via a personal access token, you'll simply be missing the first option.

GitLab.com or GitHub integration enabled

If you have GitHub integration enabled or are using GitLab.com and click the first **List your GitHub repositories** button visible on the page, you'll be taken to a page that asks you to authorize GitLab to access your account. It'll also show you all the data requested by GitLab, as you can see here:

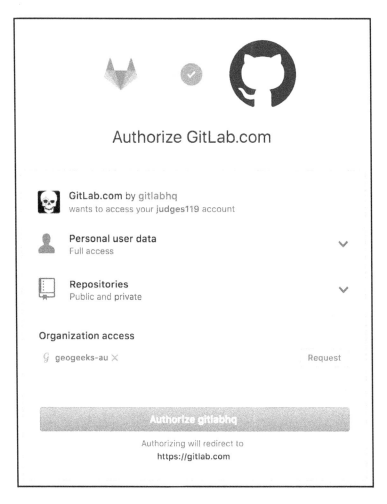

Click the authorize button and the OAuth flow will redirect you back to GitLab.

Personal access token

If you don't have GitHub integration on your GitLab instance, are not using GitLab.com, or don't want to go through the OAuth flow for accessing your GitHub account from GitLab, you can also choose to use a personal access token from GitHub. This is so it can list repositories and you can choose which ones to import from. To get your personal access token, go through the following steps:

1. Go to `https://github.com/settings/tokens` (you might need to log in to do this), and you'll be faced with the following page:

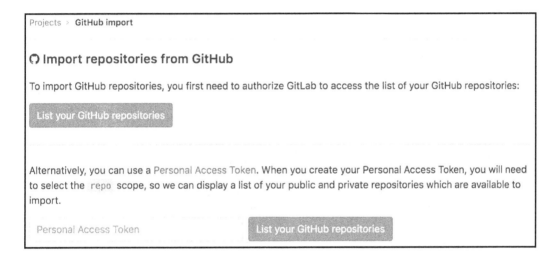

2. Click **Generate new token** to be taken to the **New personal access token** page. It should look as follows:

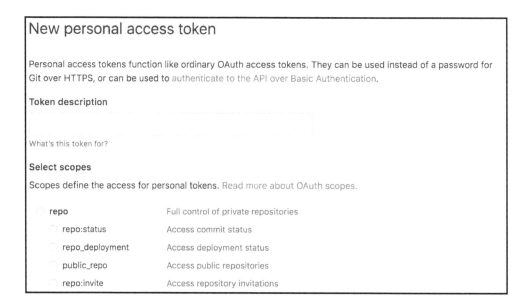

3. Give it a relevant description such as **GitLab Importer** and then tick the checkbox next to **repo**. Then, click **Generate token**. You'll be shown your new personal access token. Please copy this down, as once you move away from the following screen, you won't be able to view it again. I've included a screenshot of this view (with my personal token obscured) as follows:

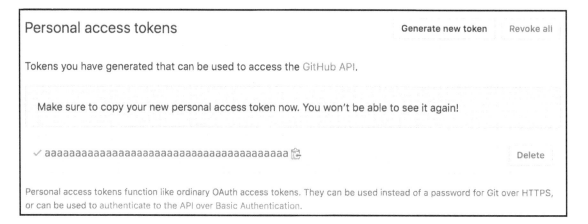

4. Now, go back to the GitLab page, paste in your personal access token, and click **List your GitHub repositories**.

Importing repositories

Now, you'll be faced with a list of not just all your public and private repositories, but also the repositories in all the groups to which you belong. These are shown here:

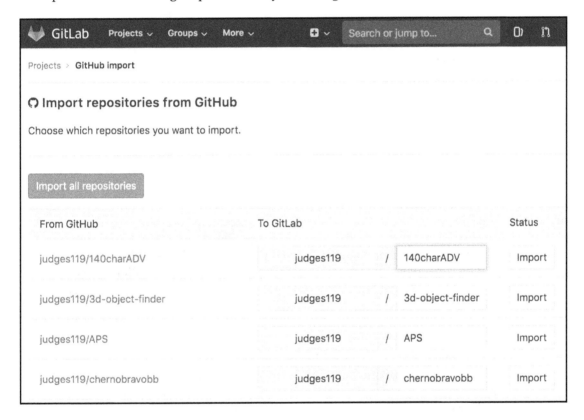

You can choose to **Import all repositories** using the button at the top, or you can import individual repositories using the button to the right of each row. You can also change which user/group the repository will belong to and rename it if you want. Please note that when you click **Import**, the process begins and runs automatically. Once it's done, the repositories you imported should be available on the GitLab home screen.

What's important to note is that GitLab doesn't just import the Git repository; it also imports the following:

- Repository description
- Issues, including comments
- Pull requests (now merge requests), including comments
- Wiki pages
- Milestones
- Labels

BitBucket

BitBucket is another popular code-hosting platform, run by Atlassian, who you may know of for their famous Jira issue tracking and project management software. Thankfully, GitLab can import Git projects directly from BitBucket. Please note that if you run your own GitLab instance (rather than using GitLab.com), you'll need to enable OAuth integration, which is beyond the scope of this chapter, but the GitLab online help can assist you with this. Once you've enabled OAuth integration – or if you're using GitLab.com – you can follow these steps:

1. From the main screen, click the + icon up the top and then select **New Project.**
2. On this page, select the **Import project** tab.
3. On this tab, select **BitBucket Cloud** and you'll be taken to an OAuth2 confirmation page (visible in the following screenshot) asking whether you'd like to allow GitLab to access your BitBucket account:

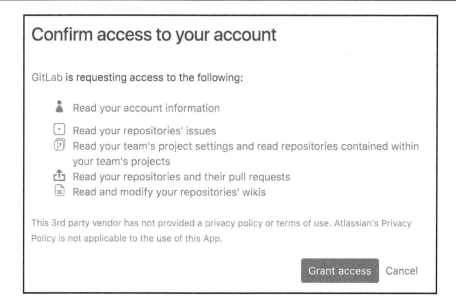

4. Click **Grant access** and you'll be taken back to GitLab, where you'll be presented with a list of your repositories that you can import from directly, as follows:

5. Now, you can choose to **Import all compatible projects** immediately, or you can import only the ones that you want to move to GitLab.

Note that you can also rename the repositories on import, as well as change the user/group to which they'll belong. In the preceding screenshot, you'll also note one repository listed as an **Incompatible project**. This project is controlled by a different version control system, such as SVN or Mercurial, and thus can't be imported directly from BitBucket into GitLab. Thankfully, there are methods of converting SVN and Mercurial projects to Git projects, which are covered later in this chapter.

Project URL

If your existing code-hosting platform allows you to check out the Git repository via a `http://`, `https://`, or `git://` link, you can also directly import the project into GitLab. This is useful if your code-hosting platform is not currently supported for full integration by GitLab. This can also be used to import public repositories that you see on other platforms and would like to make your own fork of on GitLab:

1. From the main screen, click the + icon up the top and then select **New Project**. On this page, select the **Import project** tab.
2. Select **Repo by URL** and you'll be provided with a form to fill in:

3. Up at the top, you need to fill in the repository URL, which must be preceded by the protocol identifier, such as `http://`, `https://`, or `git://` (as appropriate). If your repository is behind a basic authentication mechanism, you can put your authentication details in the URL, as demonstrated in the notes. Please note that there is a 180-minute timeout for importing repositories and anything longer than that should be done manually (covered as follows):

   > You should also fill in the project name, select the user/group for the project, provide a description, and choose the visibility.

4. Once you've done this, click the **Create project** button down at the bottom and it will automatically import your existing project. Keep in mind that this only copies across the Git data; no issues, merge requests, or other features provided by your existing code-hosting platform will be brought across using this method.

Clone and push

The least high-tech method for importing a repository is the manual *clone* and *push* process, useful for repositories not accessible from your GitLab instance or too large to be copied across using the previous **Project URL** method. In this case, you must first check out the repository so you have a copy of it available locally:

1. From the main screen, click the + icon up at the top and then select **New Project**.
2. Stay on the **Blank project** tab and do the following:
   1. Select a user/group for the project.
   2. Provide a project name.
   3. Fill out the project description.
   4. Set the project visibility level.
3. Do not initialize the project with a README. Click the **Create project** button and you'll see your new repository.
4. Now, you need to go to your existing repository that you want to import and run the following commands:

```
git remote rename origin old-origin
git remote add origin [PROJECT GIT URL]
git push -u origin --all
git push -u origin --tags
```

This will back up any existing `remote` that is named `origin` and set up your project URL as the new default `remote`. Then, it will push all the data, including all tags, to GitLab.

Moving from another version control system

You may also be in a situation where you aren't using Git for code version control. For historical reasons, or due to familiarity with other version control systems, your organization or project may have been stored in a SVN, Mercurial, or other **version control system** (**VCS**) repository. While different VCSes can have vastly different methods of operation, and even completely alien underlying storage models, there are some methods for extracting data from one system and loading it into another.

In this section, we'll run through a couple of the most common VCSes used today and how to convert to Git (and GitLab) from them.

Subversion

One of the most common alternative version control systems is SVN, which works in a client-server model that differs from the distributed model that Git provides. This doesn't mean the end times though, as there are tools you can use to convert an SVN repository into a Git one. The following steps run through the use of one such tool:

1. Ensure that Ruby is installed on your machine.
2. Install `svn2git` by running the following:

   ```
   sudo gem install svn2git
   ```

3. Run the following command to download the repository and convert it to a Git repository with all the correct branches and tags:

   ```
   svn2git https://example.com/path/to/svn/repo
   ```

4. Create a new GitLab project.
5. Run the following commands to push the Git repository to the GitLab project:

   ```
   git remote rename origin old-origin
   git remote add origin [PROJECT GIT URL]
   git push -u origin --all
   git push -u origin --tags
   ```

There are a number of different options that can be used in the `svn2git` command, which are applicable in various situations.

If your SVN repository is password protected, you can specify a username and password on the command line to allow it to authenticate, as follows:

```
svn2git https://example.com/path/to/svn/repo --username=[USERNAME] --
password==       [PASSWORD]
```

If your SVN repository contains multiple different projects, you can specify which one you want to convert with the following command:

```
svn2git https://example.com/path/to/svn/repo/nested_project -----no-
minimize-url
```

One other issue with this migration pathway is that it doesn't match up author information. If you want to keep author details, you'll need to extract the unique usernames from the remote repository with a command such as the following:

```
svn log --quiet https://example.com/path/to/svn/repo | grep -E
"r[0-9]+ \| .+ \|"        | cut -d'|' -f2 | sed 's/ //g' | sort | uniq
```

Save the output of that command, and then you need to match up every username in the list to a corresponding email address. Make sure this is in a plain text file; the contents should look something like this:

```
adam.ogrady = Adam O'Grady <adam.ogrady@example.com>
snowy = Snowy <snowy@example.com>
```

Now, you can run `svn2git` with an extra flag that points to your file with the list of authors, and it will do the conversion and map all the SVN users to git users. An example of that command is shown here:

```
svn2git https://example.com/path/to/svn/repo —authors ~/authors.txt
```

Mercurial

Another common VCS in use today is Mercurial, which has a similar focus on distributed capabilities to Git, but with some differences. Thanks to a lot of similarities with Git, it's not too hard to convert an existing Mercurial repository to a Git repository and then upload it to GitLab:

1. First, you'll need to clone the `hg-fast-export` tool:

   ```
   git clone https://github.com/frej/fast-export.git
   ```

2. Then, clone the repository you want to upload to GitLab:

   ```
   hg clone [REPO URL] mercurial-repo
   ```

3. Because Mercurial is more lax with the content it allows in the author field, you need to clean up the authors and create an author mapping file. First, run the following commands:

   ```
   cd mercurial-repo
   hg log | grep user: | sort | uniq | sed 's/user: *//' > ../authors
   ```

4. If all the usernames in the `authors` file are in the form *Full Name* `<email@example.com>`, then you don't need to do anything. Otherwise, you need to map them all to the Git format in the code file like so:

   ```
   "adam"="Adam O'Grady <adam.ogrady@example.com>"
   "snowy@localhost"="Snowy O'Grady <snowy@example.com>"
   "shmouf <shmouf@example.com>"="Shmouf Shmouflon <shmouf@example.com>"
   "adam o'grady <adam <AT> example <DOT> com>"="Adam O'Grady
   <adam.ogrady@example.com>"
   ```

5. Now, we can create our Git repository in a blank folder:

   ```
   cd ..
   mkdir git-repo
   cd git-repo
   git init
   ```

6. Now, run the fast import tool:

   ```
   ../fast-export/hg-fast-export.sh -r ../mercurial-repo -A ../authors
   ```

7. This will take a while, but at the end you should have a Git repository with all the Mercurial tags and branches/bookmarks converted to Git tags and branches.

8. Now, you need to create a new GitLab repository and push everything to it. From the main screen, click the + icon up the top and then select **New Project**.

9. Select a user/group for the project.

10. Provide a project name.

11. Fill out the project description.

12. Set the project visibility level.

13. Do not initialize the project with a README. Click the **Create project** button and you'll see your new repository.

14. Now, you need to go to the existing repository that you want to import and run the following commands:

```
git remote rename origin old-origin
git remote add origin [PROJECT GIT URL]
git push -u origin --all
git push -u origin --tags
```

Summary

After this chapter, you should feel confident in importing projects to GitLab from a variety of different sources. This is important because in many situations you may already have an established VCS or a code-hosting platform before you look at moving to GitLab, and it greatly reduces friction in moving to a new platform if you can easily import existing work.

We started the chapter by looking at importing from the biggest code-hosting platform around, GitHub. We looked at two methods of migrating: using the OAuth2 flow and using personal access tokens. Next up, we examined BitBucket by Atlassian and how to import Git projects from BitBucket into GitLab using the OAuth2 workflow. We then looked at importing any Git repository that can be accessed via URL, as well as the most low-tech method of simply downloading an existing repository to your local machine, changing the origin, and uploading to a new blank project on GitLab.

Aside from just importing projects from other code-hosting platforms, we also looked at how to convert from two other popular VCSes. We looked at moving from both SVN and Mercurial while not losing any of the branching or tagging information.

In the next chapter, we'll look at some of the advanced features of GitLab as well as a number of features only available in paid versions.

Advanced and Paid Features 7

We've looked at many of the main functions of GitLab to help you get started using the platform, but there's a whole lot of advanced and extra features in the GitLab ecosystems. On top of all the free features, GitLab also has a tiered pricing model, where higher tiers can unlock even more enterprise-focused features to help you get the most out of your version control, continuous integration, and project management.

In this chapter, we'll look at a bunch of advanced and paid features that you can use to really kick your GitLab usage up a notch, such as the following:

- Snippets
- Wikis
- Enabling Mattermost, a chat client, in self-hosted GitLab
- Administering a self-hosted GitLab
- Issue-tracking/project-management features, including burndown charts, issue weighting, and epics
- Code features, such as merge request required approvals

Snippets

If you've come from GitHub, you're probably aware of gists—a method of sharing single files, parts of files, or even just chunks of code or prose. GitLab has a similar feature called **Snippets**, but with some extra features woven into it.

You can access **Snippets** by clicking the option for it in the menu at the top of the screen:

On this page, you can view your own snippets as well as explore other snippets available on that GitLab instance. If you click **New snippet**, you'll be faced with the snippet creation screen:

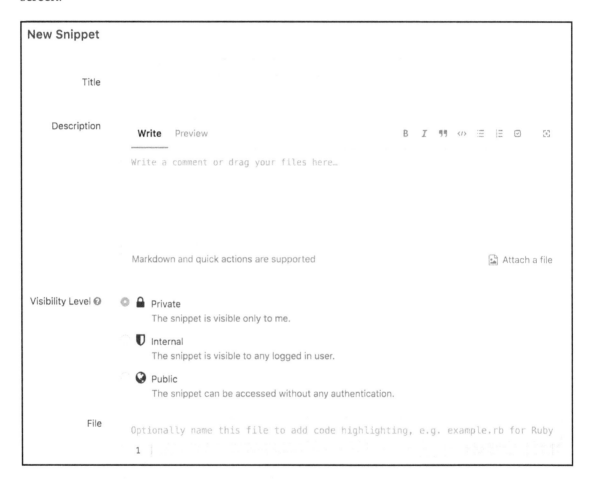

Most of the fields on this page are pretty self-explanatory; you can fill out a title for the snippet and add a description in **Markdown** format (a brief rundown on Markdowns is available in the `Appendix`). Of incredible importance is picking the right visibility level. If you want your notes to be for your eyes only, you'll definitely need to select **Private**, while the other choices allow some freedom for linking to coworkers or even interested outsiders. Lastly, we get to the main component of snippets: the file/code/writing section. Here, you can paste your *snippet* of work or even an entire file. Here's a tip: put a filename with a relevant extension (such as `.rb` for the Ruby language, `.php` for PHP, or `.md` for Markdown) and, when viewing the snippet, it will have syntax highlighting to help make it more readable. Once you've finished writing your snippet, you can hit **Create snippet** at the bottom of the screen.

When you're viewing a snippet, whether your own or someone else's, you'll notice at the bottom that there is room to both react to the snippet with a thumbs up/down or emoji as well as a space for leaving (Markdown-enabled) comments! This way, you can discuss small pieces of work or ideas without having to create a whole new repository for them:

We've covered most of the basic features of snippets, but one nifty little thing about them is that you can have project-specific snippets too! If you go to a project on GitLab, you'll see there's a **Snippets** menu item on the left side where you can collate snippets of code or fragments of information that are relevant to a project but not necessarily required in the codebase:

Next up, we'll take a look at another helpful project-based feature in GitLab: the wiki.

Wiki

Another powerful and useful feature of GitLab that mirrors some other popular version-control platforms is the option to have project documentation available as a wiki. To access this section, go to a project and click Wiki in the menu on the left side. If you haven't created any wiki pages yet, you should be met with the following information notice and a button to **Create your first page**:

Click the button to get started and create your wiki homepage. You'll notice that you have a few fields available to fill in. If you have a **Title** field available, make sure you leave it set to **home** for your first wiki page, as that's necessary for it to be jumped into when you navigate to the wiki in the project. You have the choice of formats to write your docs in, with markdown, RDoc, and AsciiDoc currently being offered.

Once you've finished creating your wiki page, add a commit message in the final box (or use the default), and then click **Create page**. Why a commit message? That's because GitLab stores wikis as their own git repository, alongside your project's git repository! On the right side of the screen while looking at the wiki, you'll have a list of all the pages in alphabetical order, as well as an option to **Clone repository**. If you click this button, you'll be taken to a page with instructions on checking out a copy of the wiki locally so that you can edit it and commit your changes. You'll need the `gollum` Ruby gem in order to properly edit and build the wiki if you're thinking of playing around with it locally:

Home · History				
Page version	Author	Commit Message	Last updated	Format
89e09518	Adam O'Grady	judges119 created page: home	10 minutes ago	**markdown**

From a wiki page, you can also check out the page history to see who made which edits and when, as well as any changes to format. This section is why commit messages are really useful, as you can write in what you changed to help others understand the growth of the document.

One last thing to remember is that guests will only have permissions to view wiki pages, so you'll need at least developer permissions on the project to make changes or create new pages.

Groups

So far, we've discussed creating and maintaining projects, issues, and merge requests on GitLab as individual users, but if you're in an organization, especially one with multiple independent teams, you'll probably want to explore the **Groups** features. You can create groups in GitLab (self-hosted or SaaS) to represent your entire organization, departments, teams, or even sets of people relating to particular products or services.

To access groups, click the Groups menu at the top of the screen and select **Your groups**:

From here, you can click **New group** and fill out the form to create a new group. Make sure you provide a name and a group path at least, however it's recommended to provide a description to give more context, as well as an avatar to help represent the group in various menus and views. Make sure you also choose the appropriate privacy settings and then click **Create group**.

You should now be looking at your new group. You have the option to create new projects for the group or, using the drop-down menu, you can create a subgroup. This is useful if you want to encapsulate teams within a department, or departments within an organization.

By clicking **Members** on the left menu, you're taken to an interface where you can invite other GitLab users to your instance. If they don't currently have an account on your GitLab instance (whether self-hosted or GitLab.com), you can put in their email address and it will send them an invite. You can also preselect their role, which is handy for ensuring people only have permissions that are relevant to their job and can't accidentally delete repositories or commit code if that's not within their duties. For temporary workers or secondments, there's also an expiration date picker so that you can create a time-boxed group membership without having to manually remove them after they've departed. Under the section for adding new members, you'll have a list of existing members, where you can modify their permissions, set expiration dates, or even remove them manually.

Also on the left menu, you'll see links (with some sub-menus) to **Issues** and **Merge Requests.** These allow you to view all the current issues and merge requests for all projects assigned to that particular group. Again, this is handy for getting a good overview of the health of a group whose work might be split across multiple projects. One notable exception is **Issues | Milestones**; if you click on that, you'll be taken to an interface where you can view milestones for all projects as well as create group-specific milestones:

You'll notice in the preceding screenshot that the first milestone is a **Project Milestone** and includes a link to the project (**140charADV**), while the second milestone is a **Group Milestone**. The difference here is that you can assign issues from multiple different projects to this milestone. This is very handy if you have goals that are spread over multiple projects, such as milestones to localize all your frameworks in other languages.

Moving projects

If you have an existing project on GitLab but want to move it to a group, follow these easy steps:

1. Navigate to your project in the GitLab web user interface.
2. In the left menu, go to **Settings** | **General**.
3. Expand the **Advanced** section.
4. Scroll down to **Transfer project**:

Transfer project

Select a new namespace

- Be careful. Changing the project's namespace can have unintended side effects.
- You can only transfer the project to namespaces you manage.
- You will need to update your local repositories to point to the new location.
- Project visibility level will be changed to match namespace rules when transferring to a group.

Transfer project

5. Select the group that you want to own the project. Please be aware of the conditions.
6. Click **Transfer project**.
7. All of the users of this project will need to update their git remote settings by typing in the following command:

```
git remote set-url [REMOTE NAME] [NEW URL]
```

The project is now being managed by the newly selected group.

Epics

If you have an Ultimate/Gold enterprise subscription with GitLab (aimed at larger businesses/enterprises), you'll also have access to **Epics**. These are a premium feature that allow you to track issues that share a common theme across different group projects and milestones. You'll find the epics section on the left menu when you're looking at a group. You can create a new epic by clicking **New epic** and providing a title, or you can browse your existing list of epics. When you view an epic, you'll notice that you can edit the title and description, as well as add a start and end date (useful for large organizational projects that have limited timeframes), as well as the ability to add group-specific labels for categorization and tagging:

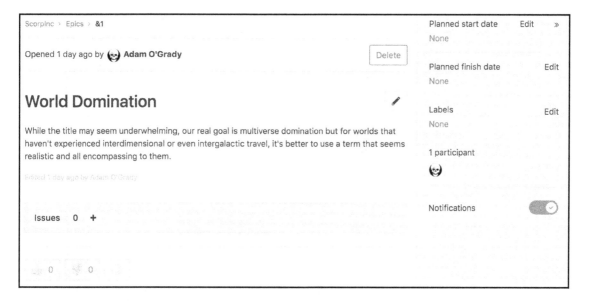

There's also a section for adding reactions (including thumbs up/thumbs down) and space for comments and discussions. The most important section, though, sits right under the description, and that's the **Issues** box. You can add issues as they crop up in the **Epic** by clicking the plus sign, pasting in a link to the issue, and clicking **Add**.

In the menu on the left, under Epics, you should also have Roadmap. This is useful if you track a lot of time-bound projects using the epics feature, as it shows you the current projected timelines for all the epics. They're automatically sorted by time, but you can choose to filter them further or even search for a particular one:

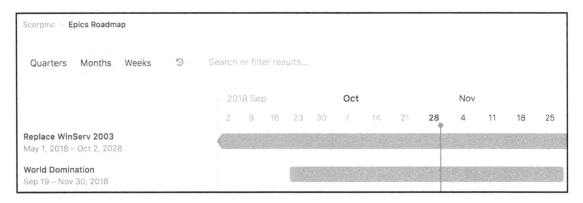

As you can see, this is a handy way of keeping track of large organizational projects and work, as well as keeping an eye on deadlines and bottlenecks. You can also track non-development projects with epics in order to keep a wider picture of organizational matters in one place.

Mattermost

One cool thing about self-hosted GitLab is that it contains everything necessary to run your own Mattermost server. What is Mattermost though? It's an open source, private chat server, similar to the commercially available Slack platform, but one that you can host yourself and have more control over. While chat servers sometimes get a bad rep in terms of productivity, they can also be fantastic for collaboration, especially for remote teams, and an excellent method of discussing topics that require more back-and-forth than an email but also need to be referred back to or searchable (unlike a phone call).

If you're running your own GitLab server, it's quite easy to enable the Mattermost service. Firstly, you'll need to have an extra domain pointed at your GitLab server. For example, if your GitLab server is reached at `gitlab.example.com`, you'll also need to point `mattermost.example.com` to the same IP address.

Log in to your GitLab server via SSH and edit the file at `/etc/gitlab/gitlab.rb`. Because of its location, you may need to do this with administrator privileges (either as a privileged user or by prefixing your command with `sudo`). Find the line that says the following:

```
# mattermost_external_url 'http://mattermost.example.com'
```

Remove the pound/hash/number symbol from the front (you can call it a hashtag if you're a millennial; no judgement) and change the URL to match the domain you created for Mattermost. If you want to use SSL for your Mattermost installation, you can change the protocol from HTTP to HTTPS and it will automatically configure it with an SSL certificate using Let's Encrypt. Now, you need to reconfigure GitLab using this updated configuration file. To do that, run the following command:

```
sudo gitlab-ctl reconfigure
```

Now, you should be able to visit the URL you specified for your Mattermost server and be faced with the following prompt:

Select GitLab Single Sign-On and you'll be taken through an OAuth flow. This takes you back to GitLab, which will ask whether you want to authorize Mattermost to access your GitLab instance data to create your account. Select Authorize and you'll be redirected to Mattermost.

From here, select to create a new team and give your team a name and URL. Now, you can get started with using Mattermost! If you've ever used Slack before, you'll be very familiar with the interface and many of its capabilities. If you have experience with IRC clients, you'll probably also recognize quite a few of the conventions and extras:

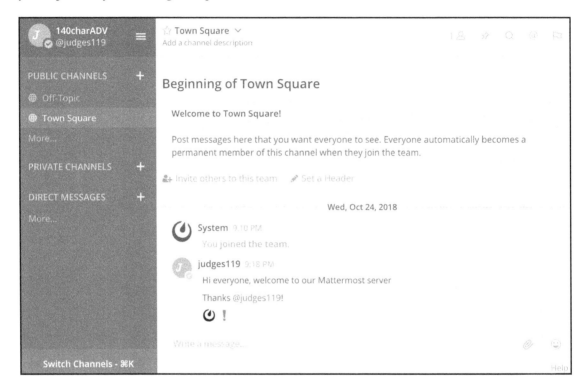

You can create public channels and private channels, as well as directly message other users. You can share files or post image, and you can *react* to messages using built-in or custom emojis. All in all, this is a very handy tool for collaboration, team bonding, and information sharing.

Self-hosted administration

If you're hosting your own GitLab instance, it's good to be aware of some of the key administration features that are provided. These include options to help secure your instance as well as ways of checking up on instance health and resolving any issues. To take a peek at your administration settings, make sure you're logged in with an **Admin** account, and then click the wrench icon at the top of the page:

Here, you'll be faced with the dashboard, which gives you a good overview of your instance, including some basic statistics, a list of popular/powerful features and whether they're enabled, as well as a summary about the different components of GitLab.

In the left menu, select **Messages**, and you'll be taken to a panel where you can create messages that are broadcast to all logged in users for a period of time. These are useful to notify users of scheduled maintenance periods, potential outages, or new features/integrations/services:

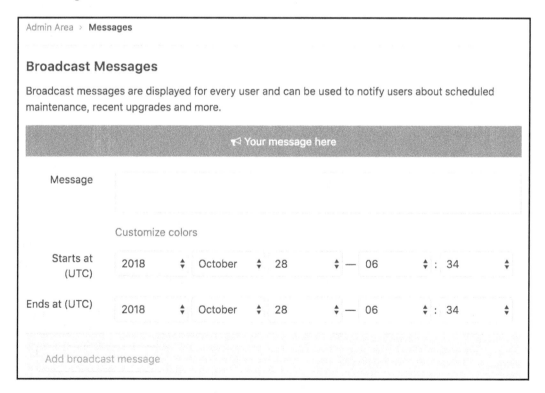

On the left again, select **Applications** to get an overview of which OAuth applications are currently authorized on your instance. This is handy for checking which applications users are connecting to their GitLab accounts and allows you some measure of auditing. You can **Destroy** authorizations that are potentially harmful or no longer used; via the **Edit** option you can change their settings, including making them automatically authorized for any new users who use the application. Of course, if you don't want users to authorize any applications, you can disable this in the **Administration** settings, which we will investigate now.

By clicking **Settings** in the left menu from the **Admin Area**, you can view all the different UI settings that make up a GitLab instance and you can modify them to personalize, lock down, or enhance your instance. Next to each section, click expand to get a better look at the different options it offers.

Under **Visibility and access controls** are some simple settings about default privacy levels for projects, snippets, and groups, but above that you have **Default branch protection**. This is super handy for setting instance-wide behavior for each project's default branch. Typically, this refers to the master branch but can be customized through a project's settings page. By changing the protection level, you can limit who has the ability to push to the primary branch (especially handy if it is an automatically deployed branch) as well as prevent people from deleting the branch or limiting who can make merge requests to it. Further down, you can also set some security options regarding git operations, such as disallowing HTTP/HTTPS and limiting the types of SSH keys that can be used on the instance to prevent weaker encryption standards being used. This is especially handy if your organization has mandated or government-regulated standards around encrypted communications.

Under **Account and limit**, some of the useful settings include **Default project limit**, which is handy if you run a public instance and don't want people abusing your service by creating and hosting too many projects. You can also limit attachment sizes for a similar reason and prevent users from registering any OAuth applications that they want.

Next up, we have sign-up restrictions. This is probably one of the first setting areas you'll want to manage after you create a new instance. You can disable sign-up entirely if you have an internet-facing instance and don't want new users coming onboard before you're ready (or if you want to invite users manually). You can also require confirmation emails to ensure any sign-ups own the email address they're signing up from. This feature requires you to have an email provider and manually change the configuration on the server, which is outside the scope of this book, but GitLab's online documentation can walk you through it. If your instance is for use by a particular organization, you can also whitelist the email addresses that are allowed to prevent other people joining, or you can blacklist signups from domains that you've had problems with before.

If you have the time, it can be worth exploring the other sections too, as there are many settings available to customize your instance. Keep in mind that many of these advanced settings can heavily change the way GitLab runs, so be wary of changing anything unless you're sure of what it does.

Next up, let's explore some of the paid features related to issue tracking and project management.

Issue tracking

So far, we've gone through the basic life cycle of issues and how to create them, but if you upgrade to an enterprise subscription to GitLab, you can gain access to advanced features that can help you manage projects with greater efficiency. Tools such as related issues, burndown charts, and issue weighting can all be used to improve your workflow and power up your team.

Related issues

If you're managing a project with many users, especially a public-facing project, you're probably used to users creating issues before checking for any similar issues that are already open or issues that may appear unrelated but have a similar cause. Thankfully, GitLab's Starter/Bronze level of enterprise subscription contains related issues:

With a Starter/Bronze enterprise subscription (or higher), you'll now see the **Related issues** box under the issue text. Click the plus symbol at the end and you'll be faced with a box where you can enter in related issues:

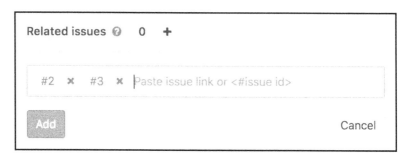

You can either paste a link to the issue or enter the issue ID preceded by a hash/pound/number/hashtag symbol. If you press a space after entering in an issue, it'll temporarily save that one and allow you to keep entering in other related issues. Once you're done, click **Add**, and all the related issues will be displayed in that box. This tool is bidirectional, meaning if you save a related issue, on that issue you'll also find a link back to this issue. There'll also be a small, colored symbol (with mouseover text) to let you know whether the related issues are open or closed.

Issue weights

If you're following the Scrum framework for managing a project or even just looking for a way to understand the amount of work required for tasks, the issue-weighting (sometimes known in other systems as story points) feature available to Starter/Bronze enterprise subscribers is probably right up your alley.

When you go to create a new issue, under Labels you should now have an option to include an issue weight—this can be any number from **0** to **20**:

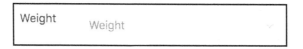

If you don't agree with an existing issue weight or would prefer it to be added during a sprint setup meeting, you can modify the issue weight in the menu on the right:

Now, when you look at the issue board, you should be able to see all the issue weights listed next to the scales icon. You can also choose to search based on an issue weighting (or search for all that don't have a weight attached) as well as sort them based on their issue weights:

You'll see these weightings when you look at an issue board, and also see the total of them when looking at a milestone, which can be helpful if you're using them to encapsulate a sprint of work and want to know how much should be possible to complete within a sprint.

Burndown charts

Another project management tool that's popular with the Scrum framework, burndown charts are a great way of tracking how much work has been completed over a period of time.

They're available in a project when looking at a Milestone—here is an example:

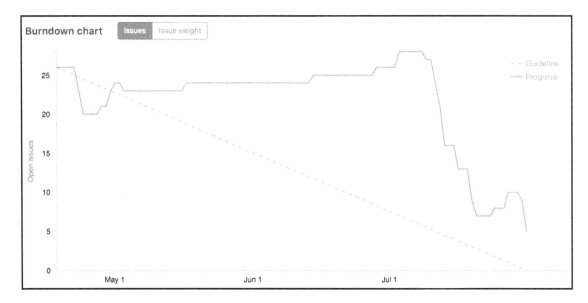

As you can see, it shows the amount of open issues in relation to the progression of time through a milestone. It shows a guideline of what progress should look like through the sprint; however, that should be taken with a grain of salt as many things can affect progress, such as weekends or breaks in a project, as well as changes in scope that force new tasks to be created. In the preceding example, you can see some early successes were overshadowed by new issues and little work was completed until early July, at which point the majority of the work was slammed through and only roughly five tasks remained open by the end of the milestone.

If you're inclined to use issue weights to track tasks, especially in environments where the complexity of tasks/features can be a huge range, then you can also view the burndown chart by issue weights, which might help reflect the work being done more accurately.

Merge request approvals

One powerful feature for high-performance teams who want to ensure all submitted code is of the highest quality is merge request approvals. This is available to all Starter/Bronze enterprise subscriptions and above. It takes two main forms, which can be intermixed:

- Requiring approval from a certain number of users before a merge is allowed
- Requiring merge approval from select users/groups before a merge is allowed

By mixing these together, you can also have combinations such as requiring a certain number of people from a particular group, or requiring at least the project owner plus one other person to approve a merge request before it can be completed. For example, you might want to allow anyone to contribute work to your backend API, but before a merge, the code must be reviewed by a senior developer or perhaps any new SVG icons require two designers to give their approval before inclusion.

When you're viewing a repository as a project owner, under **Settings** | **General** | **Merge Requests,** you'll find the following section:

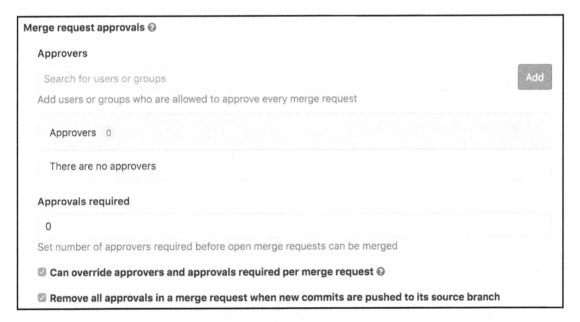

Here, you can specify a list of approvers by typing in users or groups. It works as a search suggestion, so as you start typing, the form will provide suggestions you can click. Once you've chosen a few, you can click the **Add** button to have them added to the **Approvers** box. You'll also notice the **Approvals required** box, which takes an integer value. This allows you to select the minimum number of approvals required before a request can be merged.

The first checkbox allows users to overwrite the preceding settings. This is handy if you want the settings to be a guideline rather than a limitation. The second box is a setting that will automatically remove any approvals when new work is added to the branch that is being merged. This means that if someone opens a merge request and their code is reviewed and approved and then they add more code, it will wipe those two approvals and prevent a merge until the code is re-reviewed. This is useful to prevent code being merged when potentially unreviewed work has been added.

Summary

By now, you should have a good overview of some of the advanced features of GitLab, as well as some of the paid features that can improve your efficiency and workflow if you choose to upgrade to an enterprise subscription.

We started out by exploring snippets, which are incredibly useful features for sharing or documenting small pieces of code or paragraphs of work. We also discovered that you can have them attached to your account, or on a per-project basis if they're related to a particular project that you're working on.

Wikis are another project-level feature in GitLab that let you write documentation for your project and have it hosted alongside it so that anyone looking to try out your application, library, or code can read more about it.

For self-hosted instances of GitLab, we explored how to administrate your system by looking at charts, logs, and settings available to administrators. We also looked out how to enable the Mattermost integration, which lets self-hosted GitLab users access their own private instant messaging client, designed for both private and group discussions.

Lastly, we looked at a couple of key features of paid accounts, such as *related issues*, which keep track of similarly themed problems that might come up, *issue weights*, which let you assign priorities or complexity values to various issues, *burndown charts*, which show you progress during milestones/sprints, and also *merge request approvals* which limit code being included unless it has been marked as reviewed by a set number of people or by specific users/groups.

You should be familiar with all the main features of GitLab and be ready to tackle managing and contributing to projects with it, as well setting up and running your own GitLab instance if that better meets your organization's needs. Good luck in all your future endeavors; I can't wait to see what you build!

Introduction To Markdown

Markdown overview

As mentioned earlier, Markdown is a text markup language that allows you to add common styling elements to your text with nothing more than some simple symbols. Here, we've collected some of the most common Markdown syntax for you as a guide.

One of the greatest advantages of Markdown is that the markup is readily recognizable and easily interpretable without you having to know a lot of arcane symbology and commands.

Headings

You can apply headings of different sizes to Markdown text by preceding it with the # symbol. Adding more # symbols will reduce the heading size:

```
#H1
##H2
###H3
####H4
#####H5
```

Emphasis

You can apply italics to text using an asterisk or underscore before and after the text, `*like so*`.

You can apply bold formatting to text using two asterisks or underscores before and after the text, `__like this__`.

Mixing bold and italics is done by simply having `***three asterisks or underscores***` before and after the text.

You can add strikethrough emphasis (crossing out the text) by using two tilde characters `~~before and after~~`.

By preceding a paragraph with a greater than symbol (>) you can create a block quote:

> *This is useful for quoting purposes.*

Lists

Lists are one of the simplest and best uses of Markdown, in my opinion. To make an unordered list, simply precede the text with an asterisk and a space:

```
* This is a list item.
* This is another list item.
```

By indenting with multiples of two spaces, you can create unordered sub lists as well:

```
* This is a list item
  * This is a sub-list item.
  * This is another sub-list item.
* This should be a fact about meerkats but is alas, another list item.
```

Ordered or numbered lists can be created by preceding text with a number, a full stop, and then a space:

```
1. This is the first list item
2. This is the second list item.
2. This is the third list item, it does not matter which numbers you use,
as long as the text is preceded by a number.
```

You can even do ordered sub lists in a similar manner to unordered sub lists by using multiples of two spaces before the number:

```
1. This is the first list item.
  1. This is the first sub-list item.
  2. This is the second sub-list item.
2. This is the second item in the original list.
```

Lastly, you can intermingle ordered and unordered lists:

```
1. This is the first list item.
 * This is an unordered sub list.
 * This is part of the same unordered sub-list.
   1. This is an ordered sub-sub-list.
   2. We're going really deep now.
```

Links and images

There are two ways of creating links. You can use `[inline style of link](https://example.com)` or `[reference style of link][1]`, with the link text at the bottom of the page.

You can also just use the linktext itself, `[https://example.com]`.

Inserting images looks similar to links, but are preceded by an exclamation point. Therfore, you have `![title text here](https://example.com/test.png)`:

```
[1]: https://example.com
```

Code

You can surround text with backtick symbols (`` ` ``) to represent it in a monospaced font, `like this`.

If you want to create a block of code or a set of Terminal commands, you can put three backticks on a line by themselves before and after a block of text to turn it into monospace code:

```
sudo apt-get update
apt-cache search gitlab
```

Other Books You May Enjoy

If you enjoyed this book, you may be interested in these other books by Packt:

Git Version Control Cookbook, Second edition

Kenneth Geisshirt, Aske Olsson, Et al

ISBN: 978-1-78913-754-5

- Understand the Git data model and use commands to navigate the database
- Find out how you can recover lost commits or files
- Force a rebase on some branches and use regular Git to merge on the rest
- Master the techniques required to extract metadata from repositories
- Explore Git notes and learn about the various features that it offers
- See how to decode different subcommands

Hands-On DevOps with Vagrant

Alex Braunton

ISBN: 978-1-78913-805-4

- Explore what development features Vagrant offers
- Install Vagrant and VirtualBox on Windows, macOS and Linux
- Harness the power of Vagrant to create powerful development environments
- Utilize DevOps tools such as Docker, Chef, and Puppet
- Understand everything about Vagrant, including networking, plugins, and provisioning
- Use the Vagrant Cloud to install and manage Vagrant boxes

Leave a review - let other readers know what you think

Please share your thoughts on this book with others by leaving a review on the site that you bought it from. If you purchased the book from Amazon, please leave us an honest review on this book's Amazon page. This is vital so that other potential readers can see and use your unbiased opinion to make purchasing decisions, we can understand what our customers think about our products, and our authors can see your feedback on the title that they have worked with Packt to create. It will only take a few minutes of your time, but is valuable to other potential customers, our authors, and Packt. Thank you!

Index

www.ingramcontent.com/pod-product-compliance
Lightning Source LLC
Chambersburg PA
CBHW080530060326
40690CB00022B/5086